180 MORE

DOODLE QUILTING DESIGNS

FREE-MOTION IDEAS for BLOCKS, BORDERS, and CORNERS

COMPILED BY

Karen M. Burns AND

Amelia Johanson

Martingale®
Create with Confidence

180 More Doodle Quilting Designs:
Free-Motion Ideas for Blocks, Borders, and Corners
© 2018 by Martingale & Company®

Martingale®
19021 120th Ave. NE, Ste. 102
Bothell, WA 98011-9511 USA
ShopMartingale.com

Printed in China
23 22 21 20 19 18   8 7 6 5 4 3 2 1

Library of Congress Cataloging-in-Publication Data is available upon request.

ISBN: 978-1-60468-906-8

MISSION STATEMENT

We empower makers who use fabric and yarn to make life more enjoyable.

CREDITS

PUBLISHER AND
CHIEF VISIONARY OFFICER
Jennifer Erbe Keltner

CONTENT DIRECTOR
Karen Costello Soltys

DESIGN MANAGER
Adrienne Smitke

MANAGING EDITOR
Tina Cook

PRODUCTION MANAGER
Regina Girard

ACQUISITIONS EDITOR
Karen M. Burns

PHOTOGRAPHER
Brent Kane

TECHNICAL EDITOR
Amelia Johanson

ILLUSTRATOR
Sandy Loi
Lisa Lauch

COPY EDITOR
Sheila Chapman Ryan

Contents

Introduction

It's always exciting at Martingale when we land on a concept that resonates with quilters everywhere, and *180 Doodle Quilting Designs* was just such a book. We wanted to spread the word that quilting doesn't have to be flawless and encourage quilters to release themselves from the impracticality of chasing perfection. In other words, grab those unfinished quilt tops and embrace the idea of doodling! Many of you agreed, encouraging us to share even more inspiration. And so, we present *180 More Doodle Quilting Designs*. More than a dozen talented designers have contributed beautiful doodles for you to use however and wherever you choose.

Keep in mind that doodling is anything but an act of rigid restraint, but it's also far from a mindless distraction. Whether you're doodling in the margins of paper or stitching pebbles on the surface of your quilt, doodling is associated with enhanced creativity, better concentration, and improved multitasking. The beauty is that you're achieving all those benefits while enjoying the calming act of unbridled "drawing." So, while we've provided stitch paths, enabling you to exactly duplicate each design, we also encourage you to engage your artistic license; jut off in your own lane by ignoring a loop here or a leaf there, and reroute the stitch path in a way that enhances your project. In other words, relax and enjoy the ride.

Each doodle collection of three—designs for corners, blocks, and borders—has been designed to coordinate in a single project, but as you flip through the pages, you may determine that a border for one doodle pairs just as beautifully with the corner design from another. Some, such as Spider Power (page 106) and Spiderweb Herringbone (page 108), or Searing Sun (page 76) and Flame (page 80), are obvious mates. Others, such as Boxy (page 12) and Daisy to Be Square (page 100), suggest a subtle harmony. As in the previous book, *180 More Doodle Quilting Designs* includes an assortment of lines, waves, squiggles, loops, curves, pebbles, swirls, curls, feathers, and fun whimsical motifs. And this time around we've also included a lovely bouquet of flower-themed designs that will magnify your floral prints and have your solids blossoming.

If you're new or relatively new to machine doodling, take a minute to look over the information on how to use this book. Practice on some swirls, curls, and loops of your own. The movements quickly become second nature, and before you know it, layering, backing, and finishing will become your favorite step in quiltmaking.

How to Use This Book

Not only will you find an inspiring and diverse assortment of quilting designs in this book, you'll also discover a great resource for developing your free-motion quilting skills, whether you quilt on a long-arm or a home sewing machine. Each design set includes three coordinating designs (a square block, a border, and a setting triangle) to give your quilt a cohesive look. The sets are divided into five categories so you can easily select a design that suits your skills as well as the style of your quilt.

The design sets include useful stitching tips from the designers, as well as arrows showing where to start and end your stitching. Some designs in the book have color-coded lines (black, blue, red, and/or green). These colors are meant to show separate elements of the design that have different stopping and starting points, or make it easier to follow a path that might guide you back over a previous line or element. You might stitch an outline shape first (black line), and then fill in the shape or negative space with swirls or other motifs (blue line).

Trace the Doodles

Once a set of designs catches your eye, it's time to tap into the power of doodling. While you might be tempted to jump right to stitching, doodling on paper is an invaluable step that allows you to get accustomed to the rhythm of the design and create the muscle memory you need to stitch in a continous line. It also gives you a chance to practice without the pressure of using thread and fabric.

You'll need a few easy-to-find drawing supplies to embark on your doodling adventure. Invest in a simple sketchbook with unlined pages, as well as felt-tip pens or markers. Test out a few types of pens to find one that has a smooth feel and flow for sketching. It's also useful to have a pad of tracing paper to practice doodling directly over the designs in the book. This

will help you understand the easiest stitching path to take as you follow the arrows.

Start by placing tracing paper over the design. Place your pen at the "start" dot, and then slowly trace the line following the arrows, doing your best to keep a continuous line and not lift your pen. As you trace, you'll start to understand how the design is formed, and you'll get a feel for the repetitive motion that you'll be using. Repeat this process as many times as you like, building up confidence that you can doodle the design without needing to trace it.

Trace doodles to get a feel for stitching the design.

Doodle Freehand

Next, try doodling the design freehand in your sketchbook. Using the original design as a reference, doodle the design on paper while maintaining a continuous line. Don't worry about drawing perfectly or making a pretty picture. The process of doodling is all about developing your muscle memory and

Left: *Doodle the design freehand, using the original for reference.*
Right: *Practice quilting on a sample quilt sandwich.*

finding a tempo that feels natural and relaxed to you. The goal is to feel calm and confident when it's time to stitch. Remember that it's okay if your doodles aren't an exact match to the original drawing. You'll find that the more you practice, the better your doodles will be.

Now that you're well acquainted with the rhythm of the design, it's time to graduate from pen and paper to needle and thread. Make a few small practice quilt sandwiches from fabric and batting. Use a thread color that doesn't contrast too highly with the fabric; otherwise, you might find yourself fixating on mistakes. Draw the outline of the quilting shape on the fabric to use as a framework. Relax your mind and body, lower the needle, and start stitching. Aim for a stitching speed that feels efficient without being rushed. Allow the muscle memory that you developed through doodling to guide your movement. The process is much more important than the final product, so don't focus on making a beautiful quilt sandwich. When you've filled one quilt sandwich with doodles, start stitching on another one. Once again, practice is key. Even practicing 10 to 15 minutes at a time will build your skills and you'll quickly see improvement.

Practice Stitching

Many designs contain motifs that can be stitched in different ways, so practicing will help you find a method you like best. For example, when stitching pebbles, it's possible to create them by retracing your previous circles or by stitching them in a figure-eight pattern. Or you can stitch half-circles in one direction and complete the circles in the opposite direction.

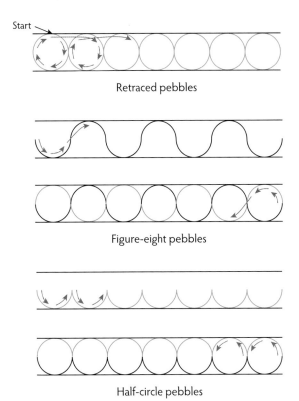

Retraced pebbles

Figure-eight pebbles

Half-circle pebbles

Play with the scale, size, density, and combination of design elements to customize them for your projects. Don't be surprised if you start to dream up doodle designs of your own, so always keep that sketchbook handy!

Spiky Feather

DESIGNED BY VICKI RUEBEL

Create a fun, modern feather that fits nicely in many shapes. The feather plumes should reach out from the edge in a smooth curve and become flat at the ends. To fill a square shape, start in a corner and build the feather from the bottom up, alternating plumes on the left and right. Drawing a diagonal reference line will help keep your feather centered.

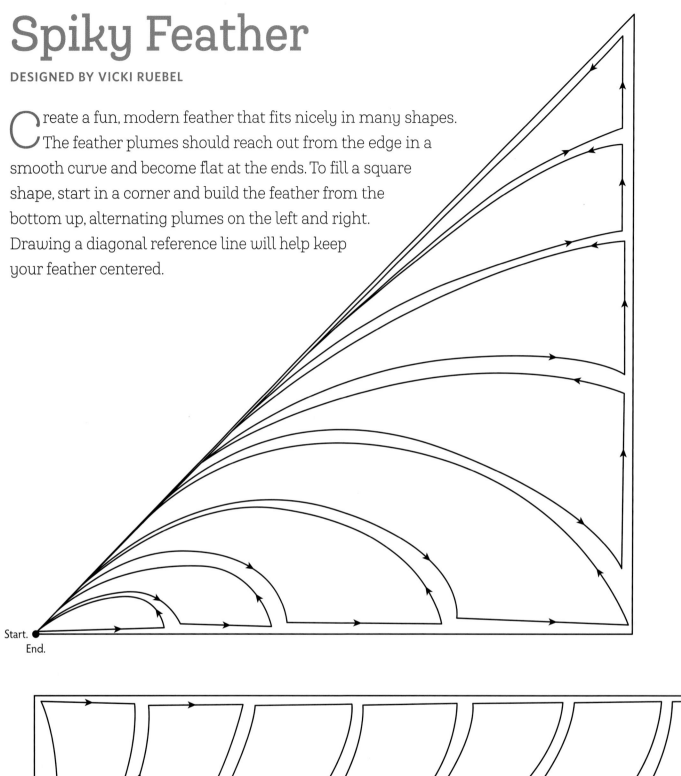

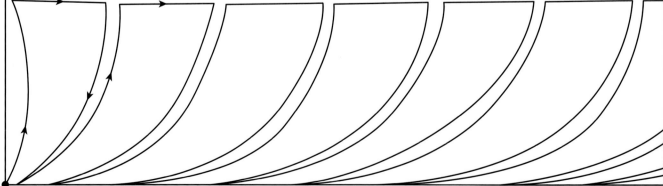

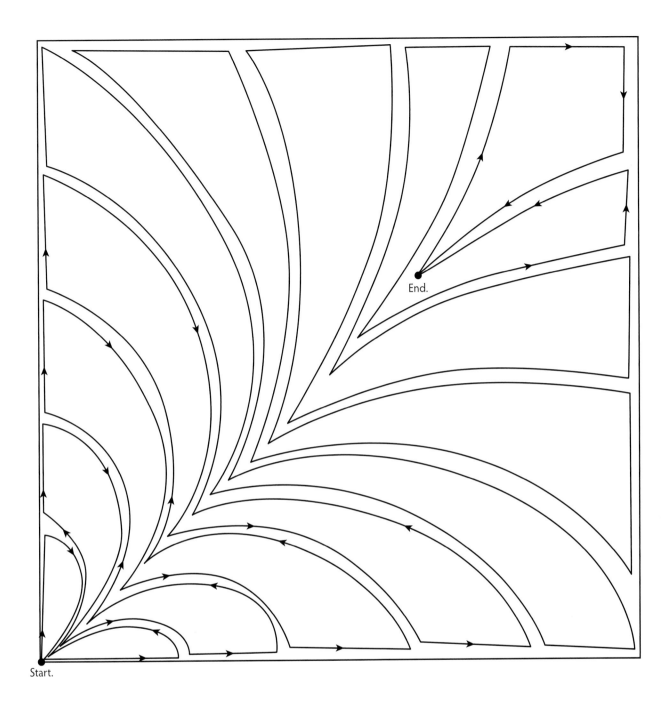

Start.

End.

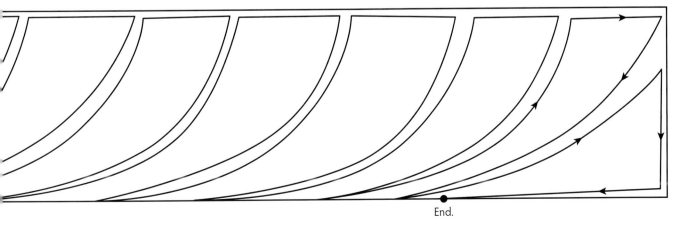

End.

Wavy Peel

DESIGNED BY MELISSA CORRY

Wavy Peel is a fun way to add variety to a basic arc. It works great in spaces filled with patchwork, such as nine-patch and sixteen-patch units, because you can easily stitch the curves from one corner of a square to another. It's also perfect for patchwork borders. When quilting it, Melissa repeats "up and down" in her head, which helps her get that wave each and every time. For the square design, follow the black stitching path first and end with the blue path. Happy quilting!

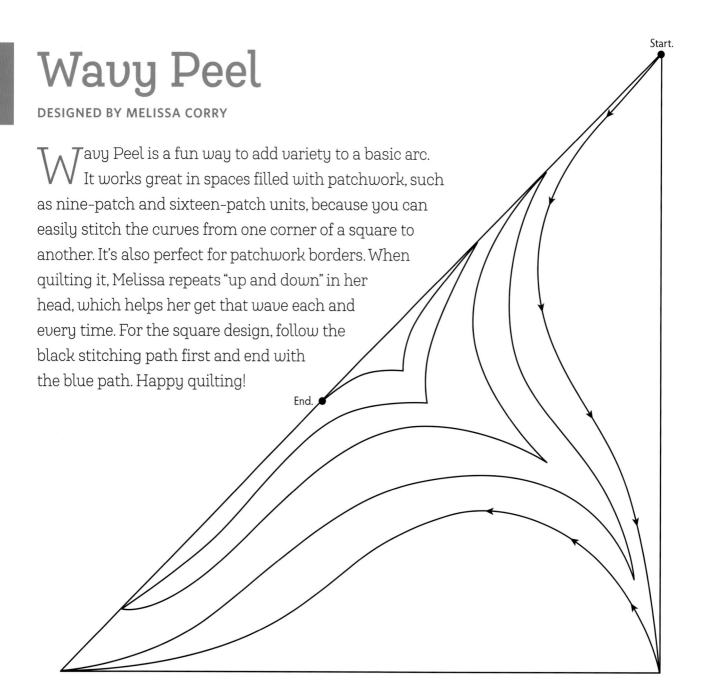

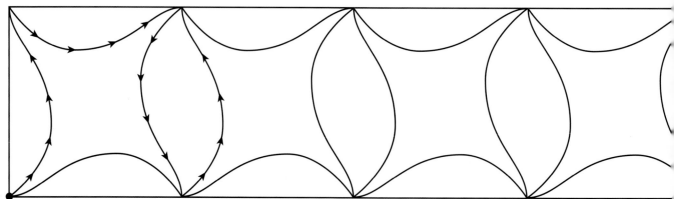

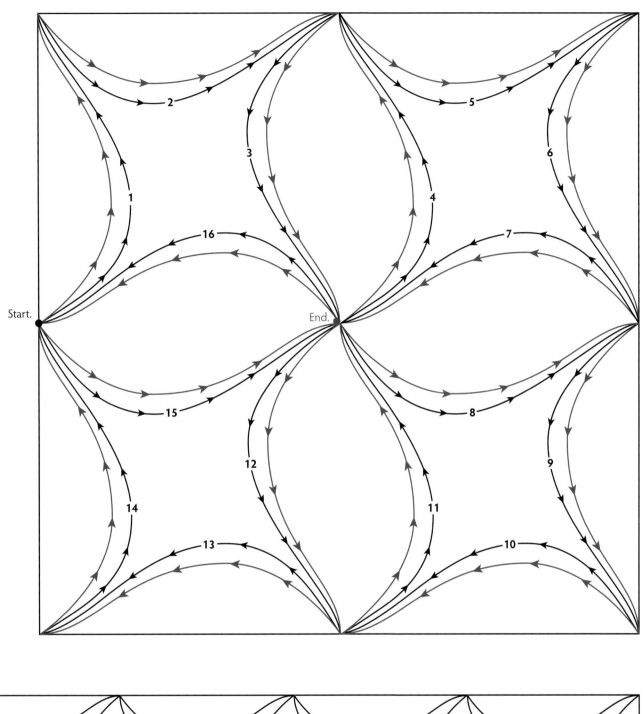

Start.

End.

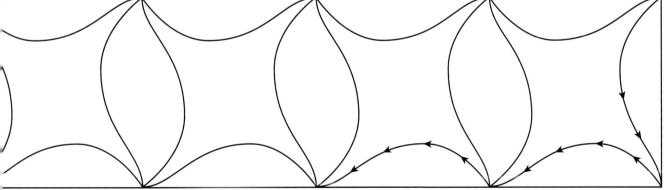

Boxy

DESIGNED BY VICKI RUEBEL

A simple design like Boxy works great in any shape. The long, straight lines extend into the shape and help define the area. Begin in the center and stitch the large triangular shapes first (the black lines), then stitch smaller triangles inside them (the blue lines). You can mark the lines before you begin to stitch to make the sections even, or you can freehand the design and not worry about perfection.

Start.
End.

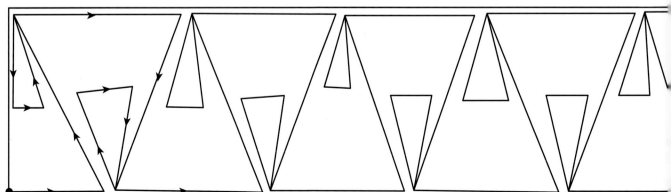

Start.

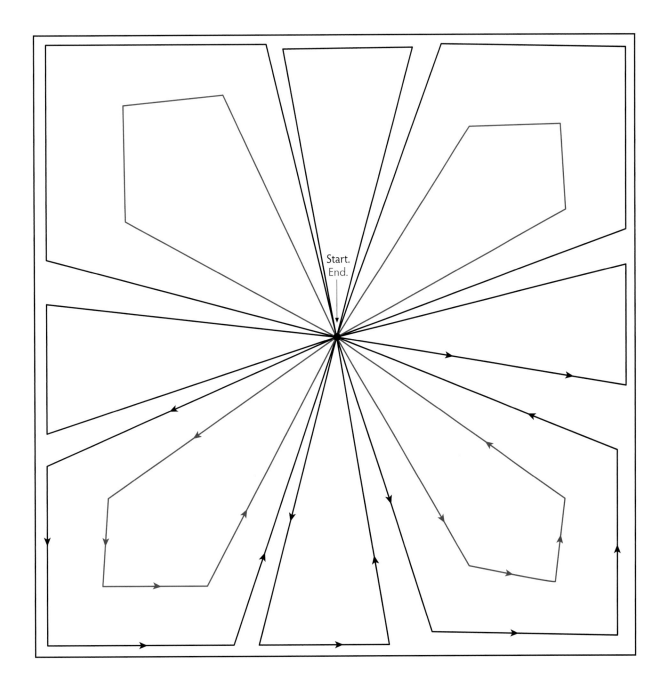

Start.
End.

End.

Jagged Puzzle

DESIGNED BY KAREN M. BURNS

The Jagged Puzzle design is an interesting alternative to a more rounded stipple. While it works on any quilt, it's ideal for a quilt for a boy or a man when you don't want something too fancy or frilly. There really is no rhyme or reason to the size and shape of the jagged pieces, so make it your own.

Start.

End.

Start.

Start.

End.

End.

Pebble Chain

DESIGNED BY VICKI RUEBEL

A fun combination of straight lines and swirly circles, Pebble Chain doesn't require any measuring. Begin by stitching a straight line and randomly add swirly circles as you go. You can swirl around the circle as many times as you'd like. The key to the design is staggering the circles in between each other from row to row, making this design ideal for filling a background or borders.

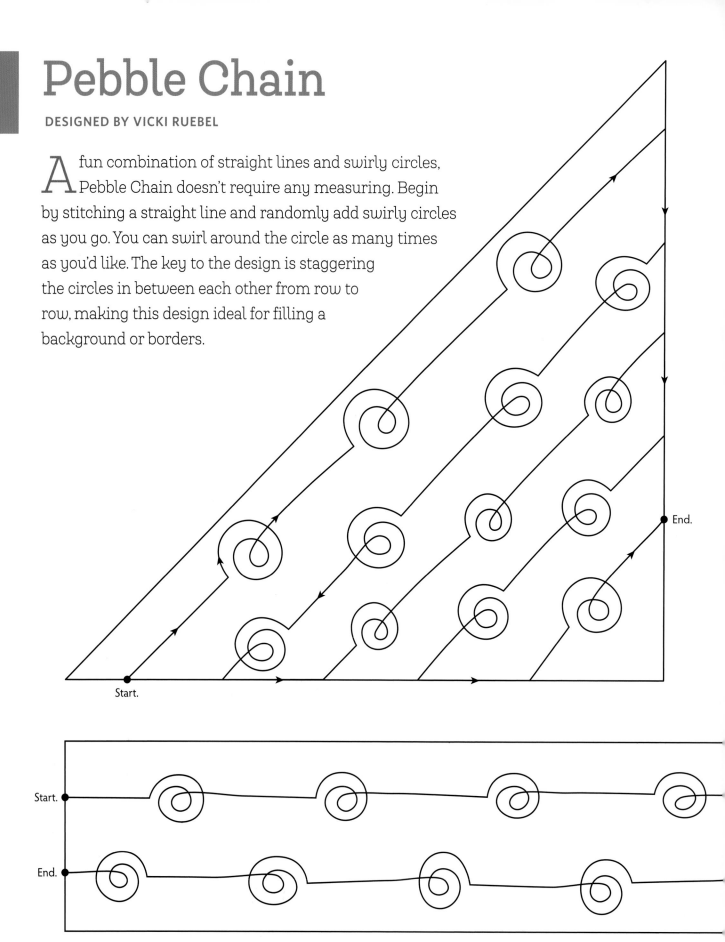

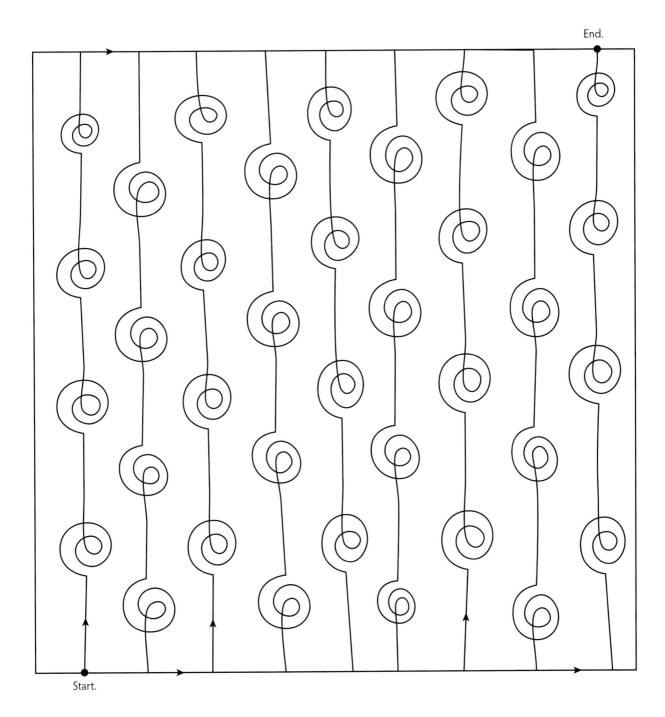

End.

Start.

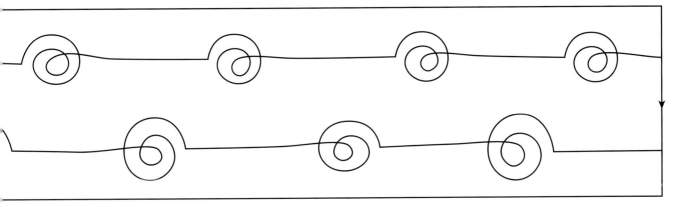

Prairie Windmills

DESIGNED BY DIXIE THUE

Prairie Windmills is a simple design that can be stitched as a full circle to fill a square or as a half circle for a setting triangle or border. Stitch in the ditch to travel from one motif to the next when stitching the setting-triangle and border designs.

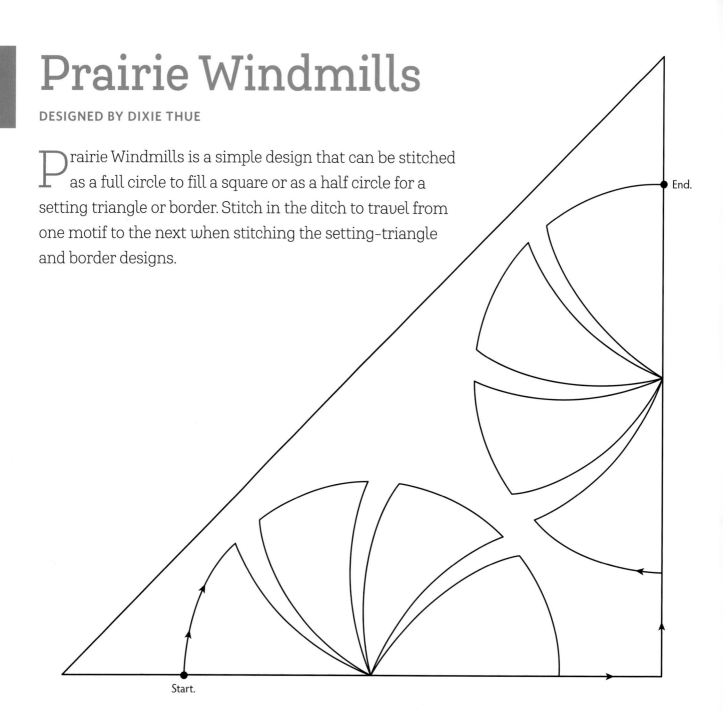

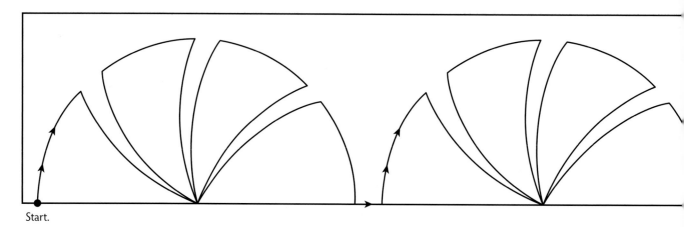

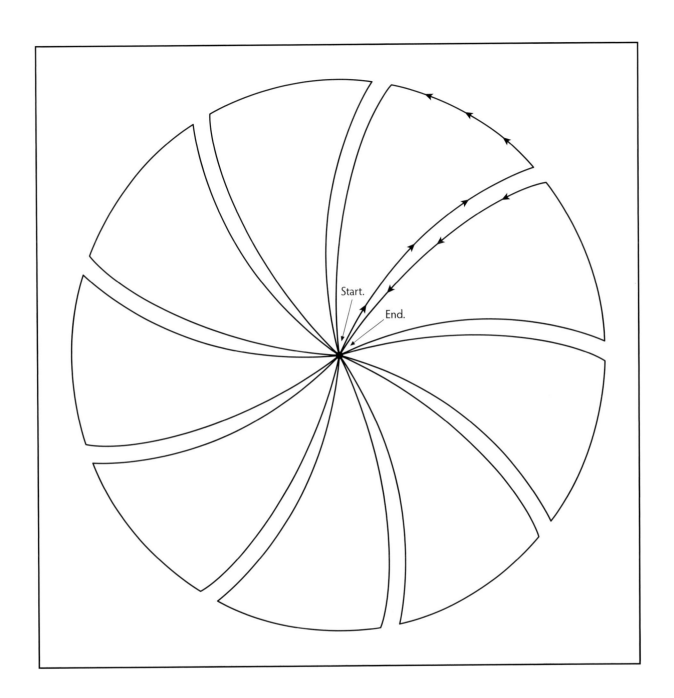

Start.

End.

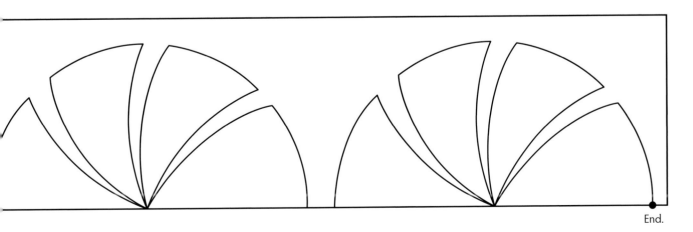

End.

Water Puddles

DESIGNED BY VICKI RUEBEL

Water Puddles is the perfect design to emulate water on your quilt. This design is very easy to execute and great for beginners. It's made up of short, straight lines combined with U-turns. Every now and then, fill in a U-turn to create a puddle for added texture. Water Puddles is great for background fills of any shape or size.

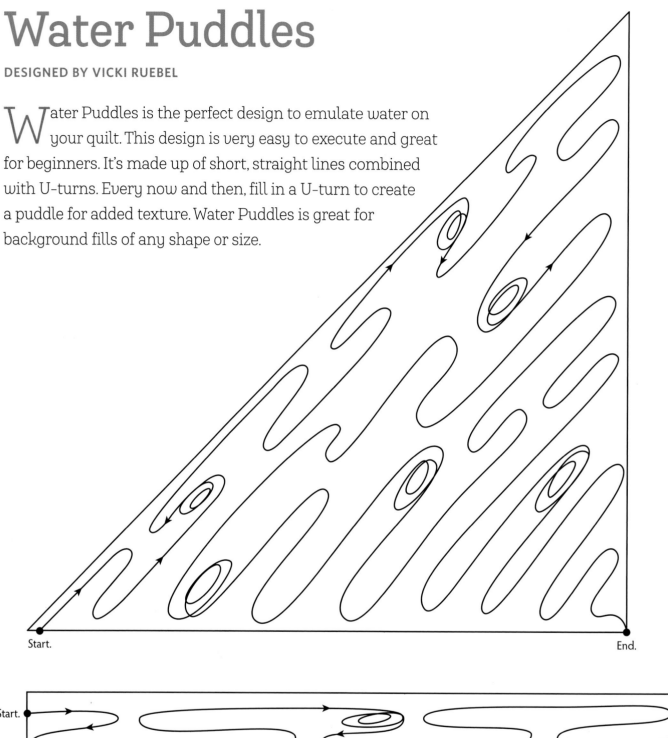

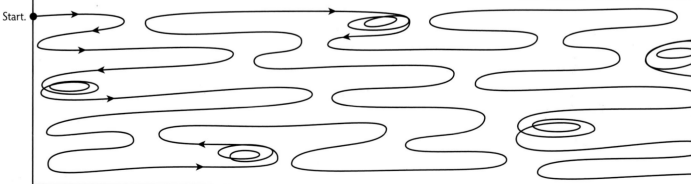

End.

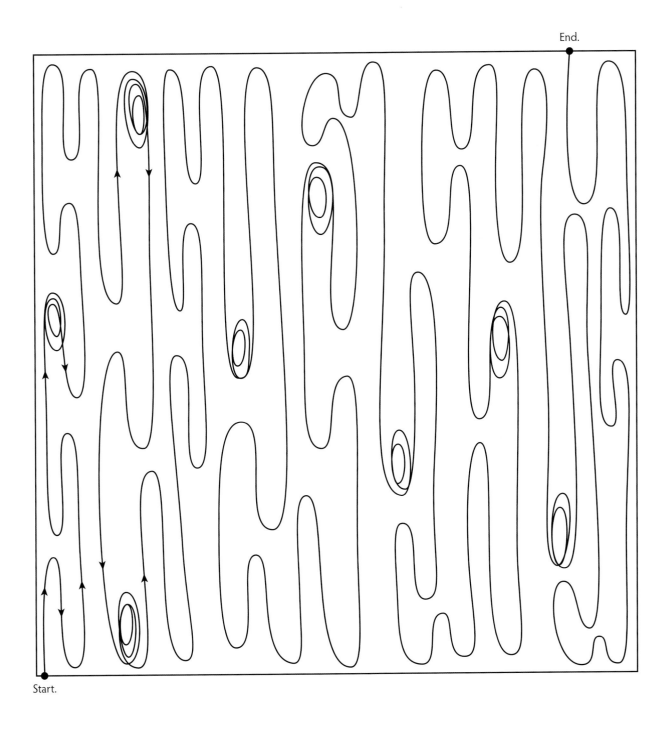

Start.

End.

Argyle

DESIGNED BY AMELIA JOHANSON

A series of lines, zigzags, and crisscrosses creates the look
of argyle in this straightforward design. Make use of the
ditches to move from one stitching line to the next, and feel
free to mark along the edges where the lines stop and
start. If you want, cheat a bit by using your machine's
quilting bar—technically it's doodling with a crutch,
but we won't tell. Begin stitching the black path
and end by stitching the blue path.

Start.

End.

Start.

End.

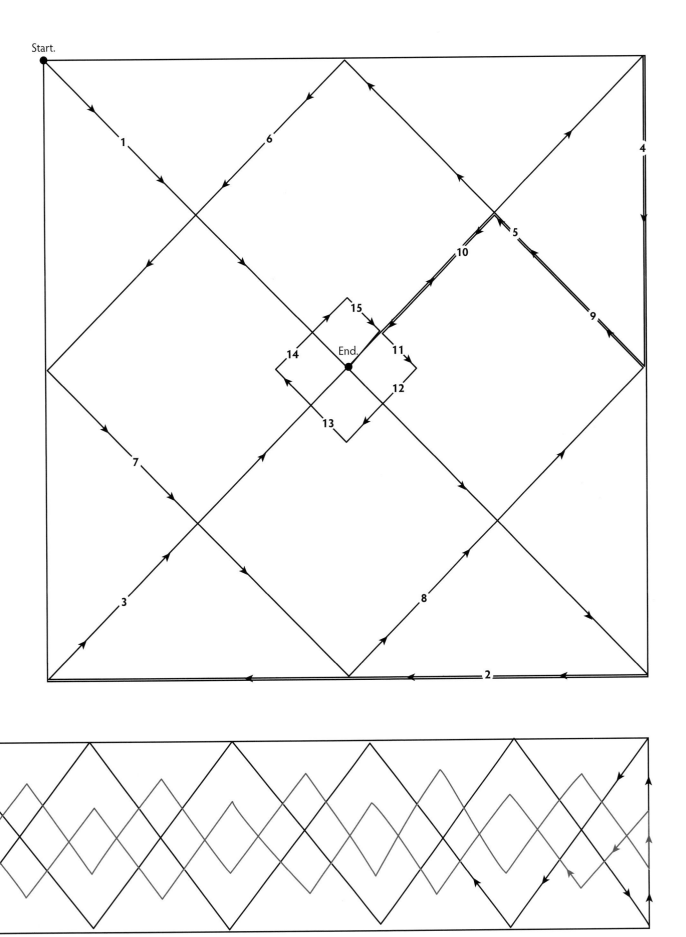

Start.

1
6
4
5
10
9
15
End.
14
11
12
13
7
3
8
2

Pyramids

DESIGNED BY REBECCA SILBAUGH

When you want a modern texture and the usual stripes just won't do, try Pyramids. You can make them as abstract or as evenly spaced as you'd like; it's all about creating long, thin angles. Bounce around from place to place using your pivot point as your anchor and add variety in the spacing of your lines to give even more interest. For the square design, stitch the black path first and end with the blue path.

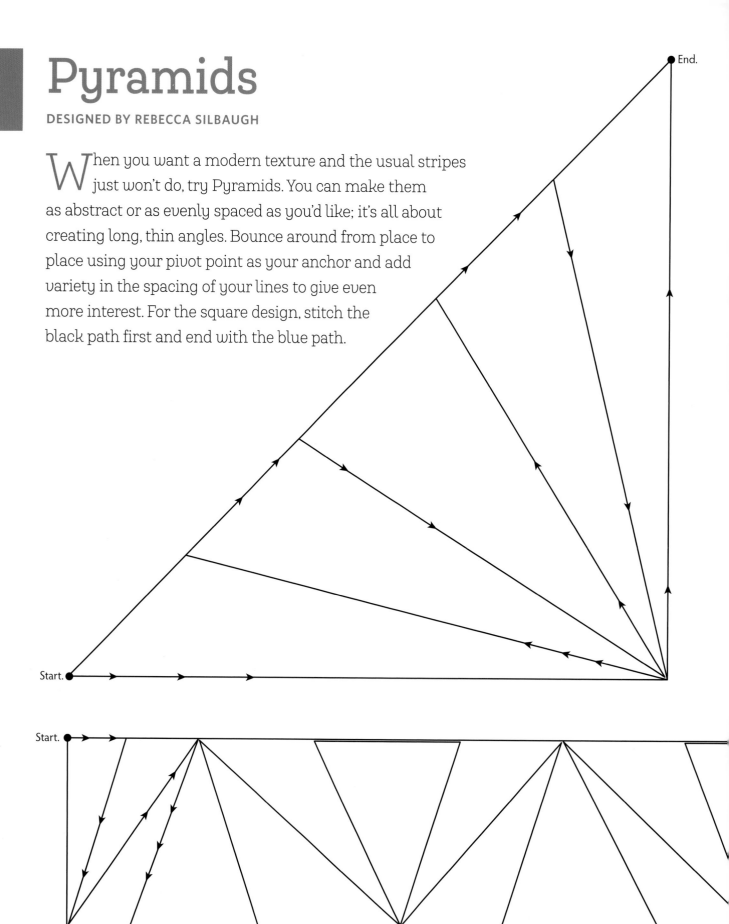

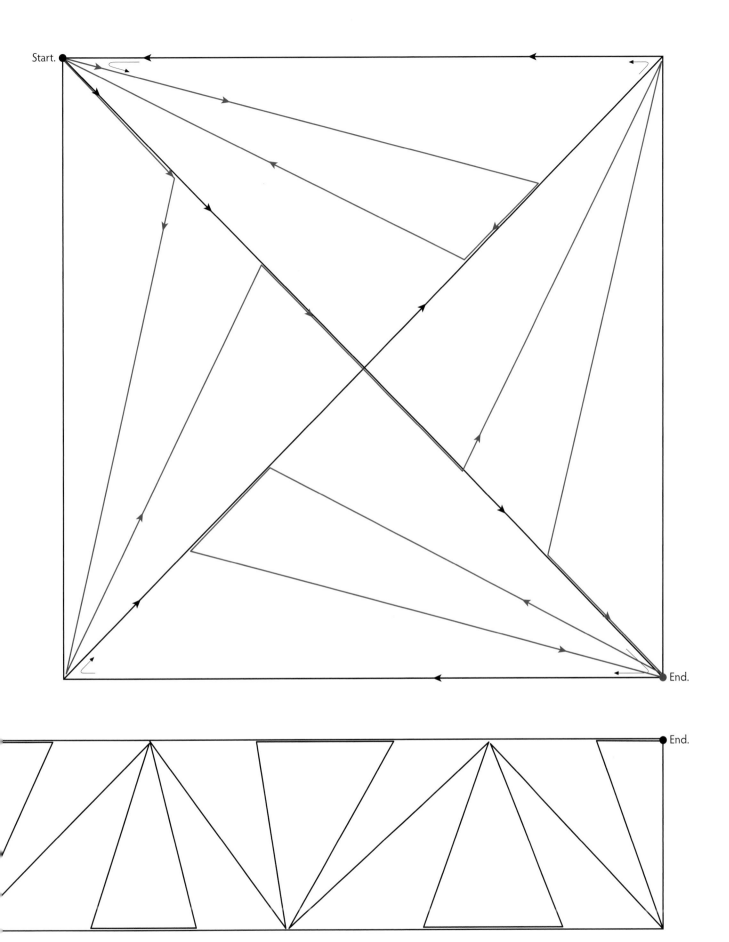

Start.

End.

End.

Herringbone

DESIGNED BY DARA TOMASSON

If you've been a little fearful of straight-line quilting, this design is a great place to start because it doesn't need to be perfectly symmetrical or straight. The lines can be spaced however close or distant you desire. The design is created through a two-step process: First, establish the vertical lines. Second, stitch the horizontal lines in a chevron pattern. Remember, practice on paper first to get the rhythm down before heading to the machine.

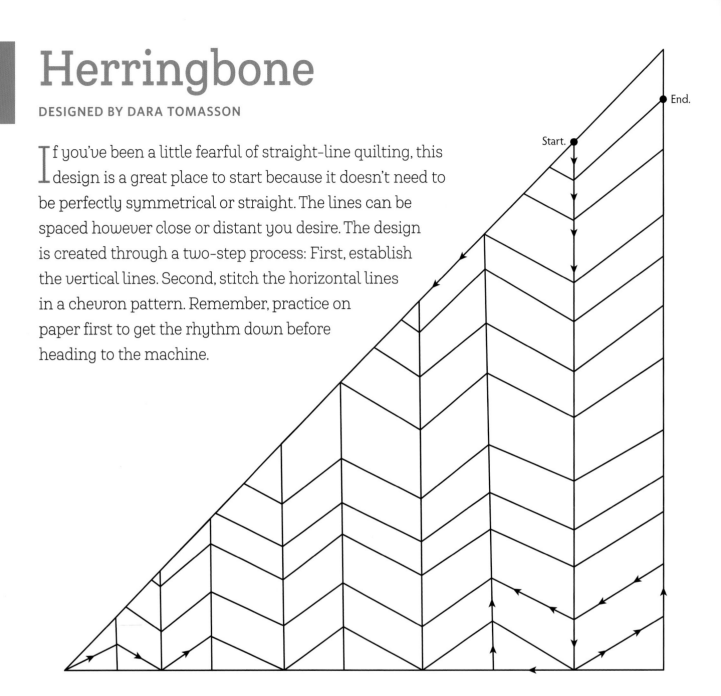

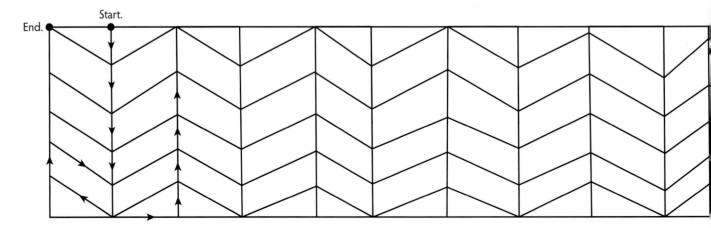

Start.

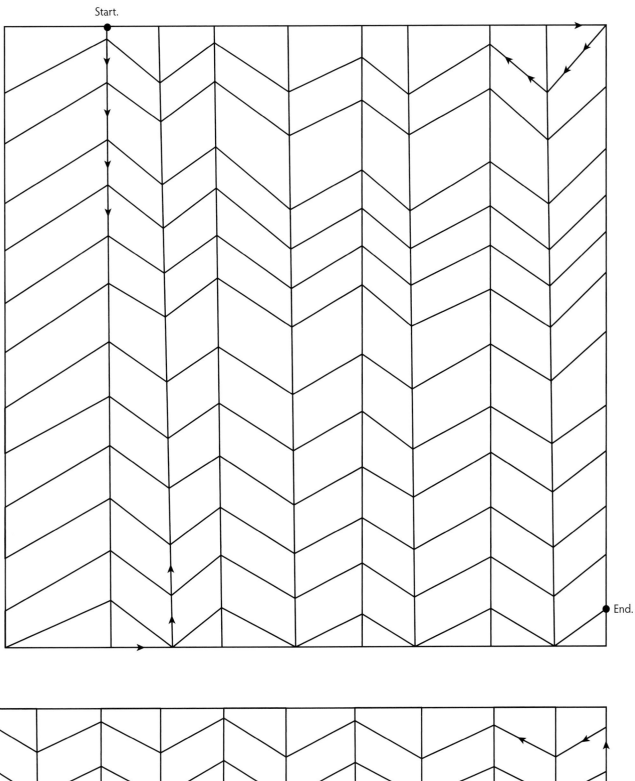

End.

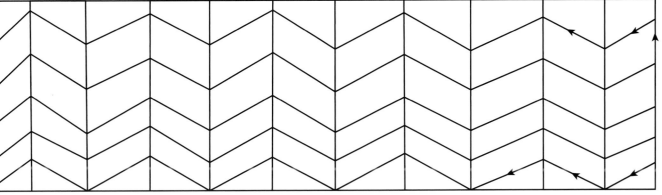

Ricochet Star

DESIGNED BY REBECCA SILBAUGH

Sometimes a design is a great chameleon, blending in with different styles of quilts like it was meant to be. Ricochet Star looks amazing on modern quilts but can also be the little something extra on a traditional quilt without being over the top. Simply quilt from one corner to the opposing center, working around the space. It's that easy.

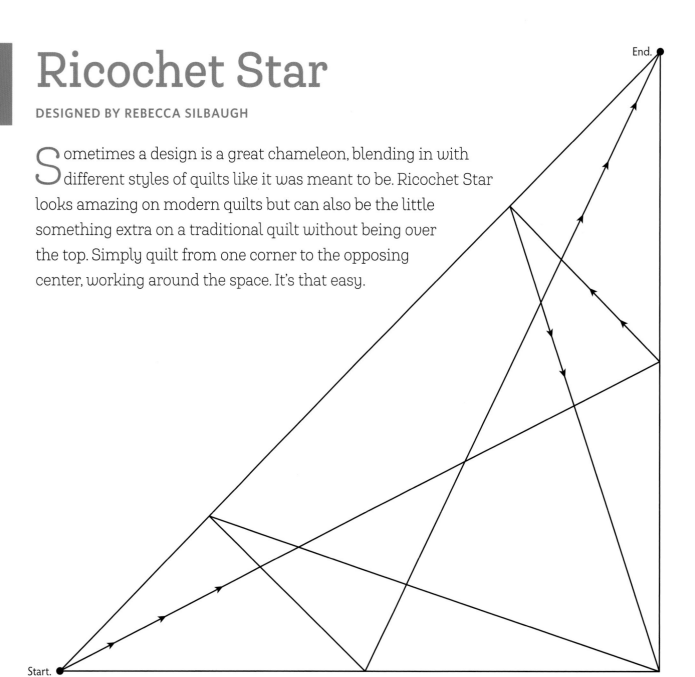

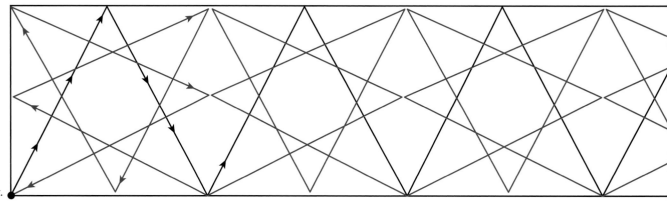

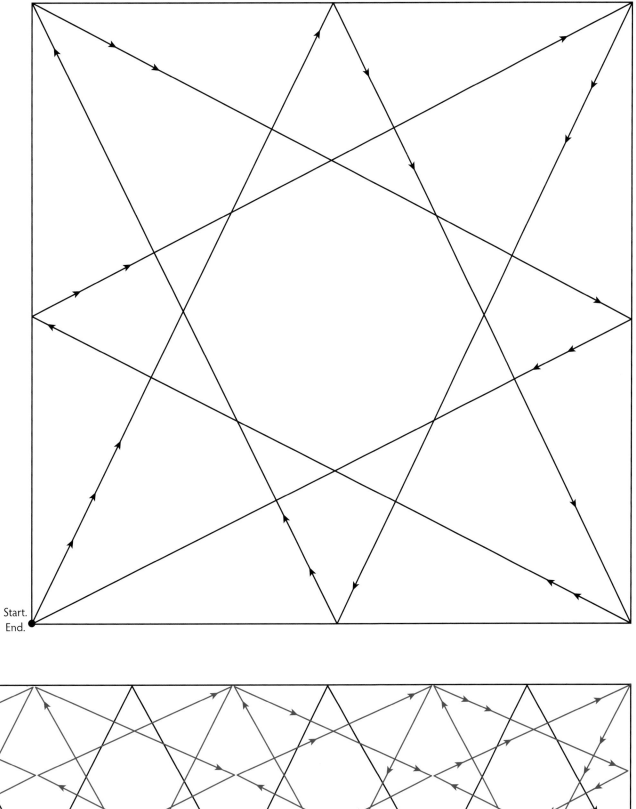

Start.
End.

Ladyfingers

DESIGNED BY VICKI RUEBEL

Ladyfingers adds a special touch to any quilt. The lacy texture is sure to please. Create the pattern by stitching small humps across the quilt. Then add the loops as you travel back to the beginning. You can add this design to any shape and fill in the background with straight lines. Measuring the distance between the lines is not necessary; why not freehand the lines for a more organic look?

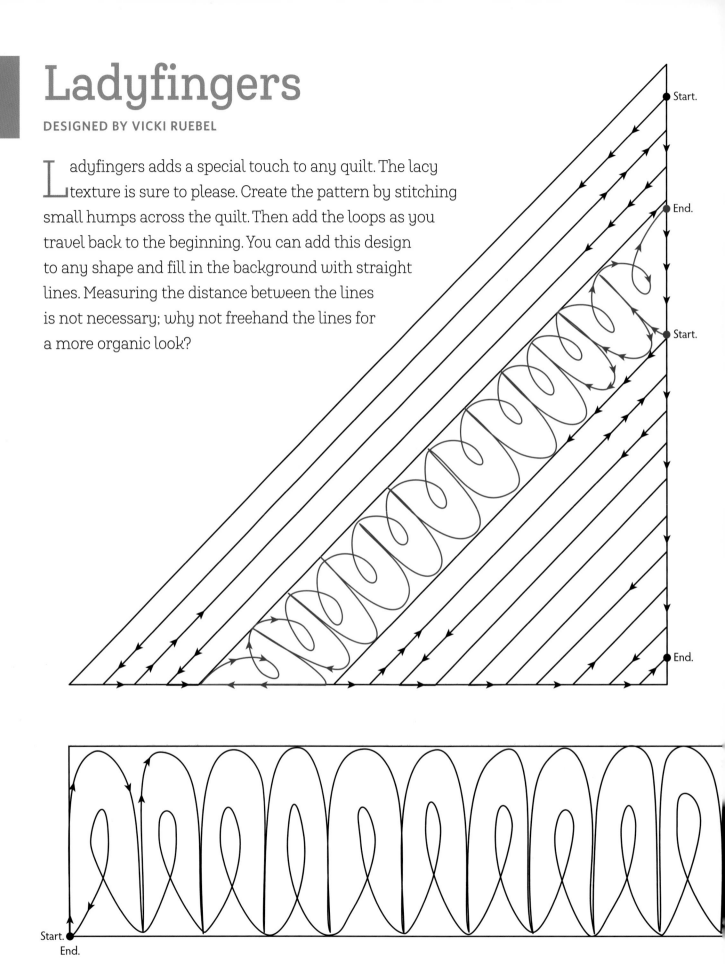

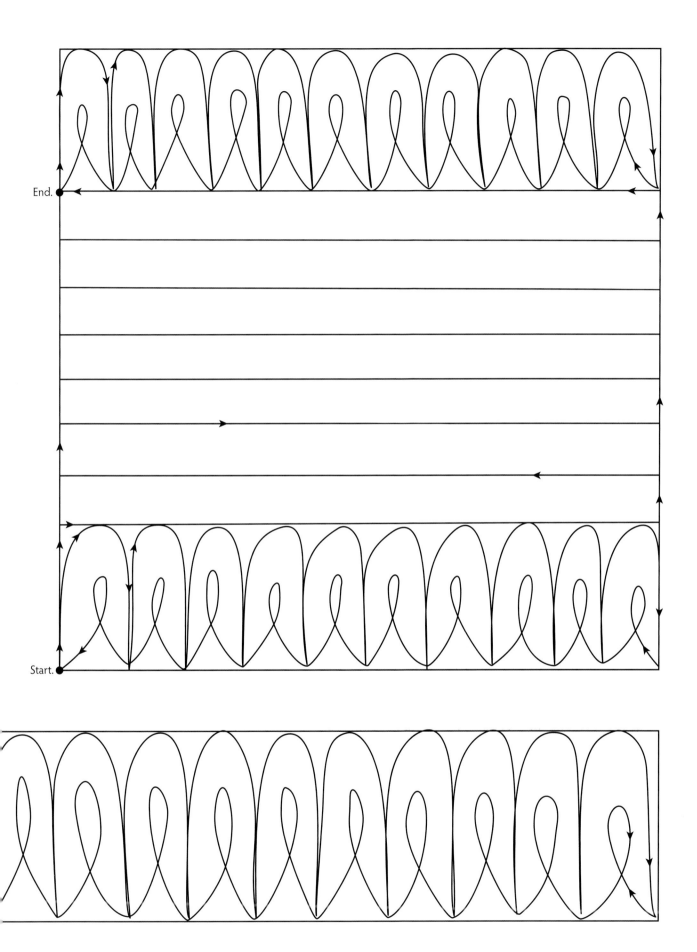

End.

Start.

Spiky Swirls

DESIGNED BY VICKI RUEBEL

Spiky Swirls features a simple swirl, capped off with a little spike that's easy to elongate and stitch into corners. Begin by quilting a slightly curved line and form a swirl. Echo the swirl on the outside, creating the spike as you go. The design works well as a single spike swirl or you can combine several to use in a border.

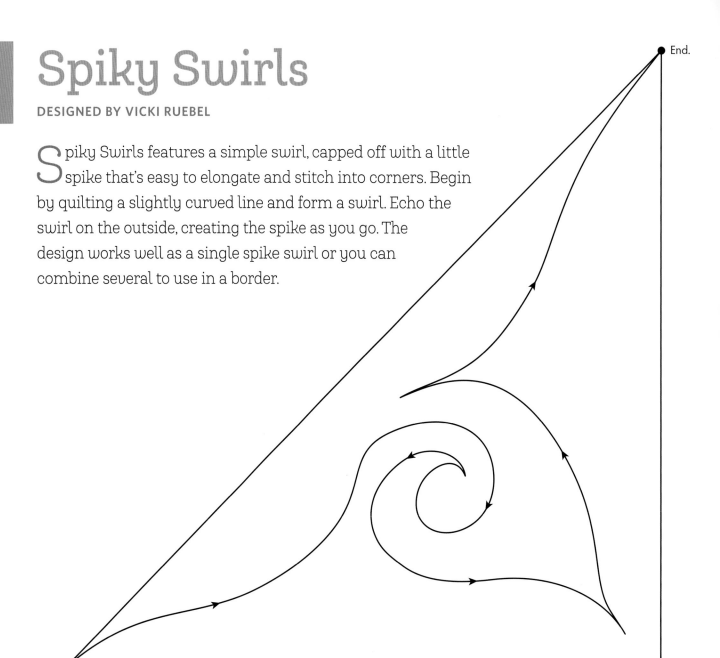

End.

Start.

Start.

Start.
End.

End.

Pebbles by the Shore

DESIGNED BY LAURIE GUSTAFSON

What a great motif to use on quilts for nature lovers! Imagine a river meandering through each quilt. The water is made by stitching loose S shapes and adding swirls to create an eddy. There is no right or wrong shape for this design. The rocks can be as large or small as you like and just the right shape to fill in your space.

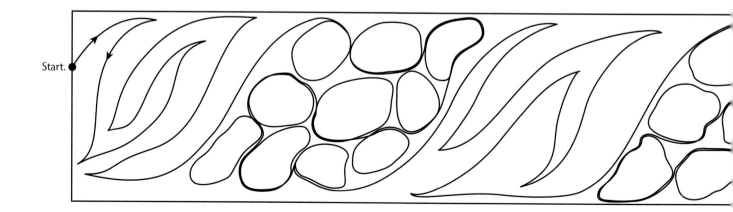

Start.

End.

End.

Double Loop Ribbons

DESIGNED BY REBECCA SILBAUGH

Rebecca loves using the ribbon candy design in her quilting, but sometimes she wants to create a little bit more interest, especially in larger areas that need to be more consistent in density. That's where Double Loop Ribbons comes in. Just adding a small circle at the center of each loop completely changes the personality of the design.

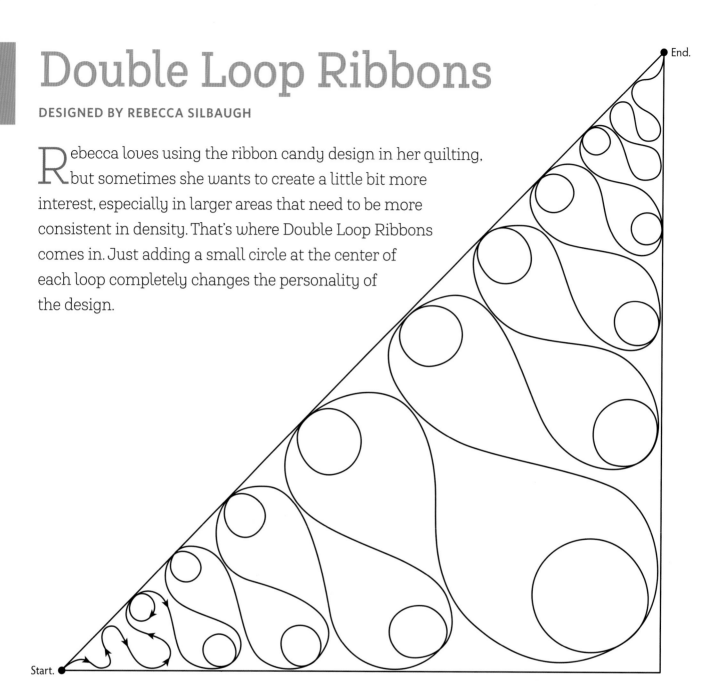

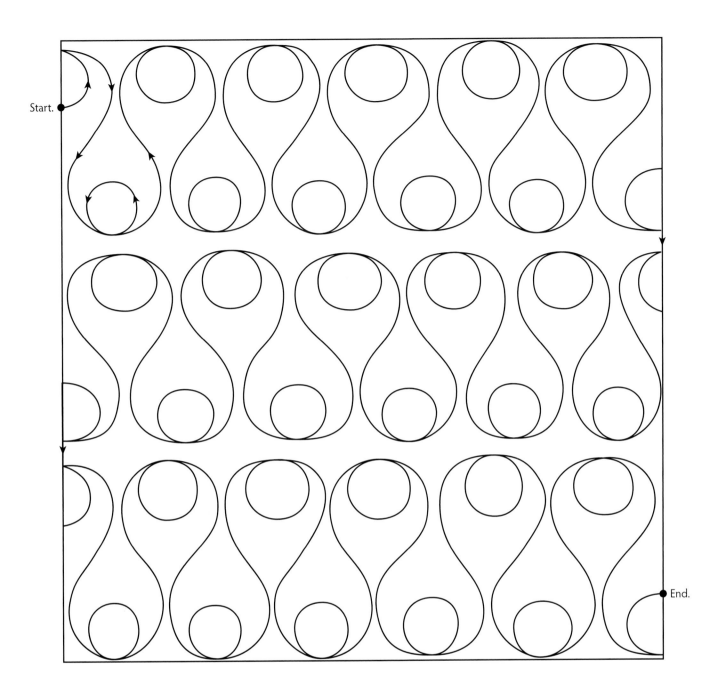

Start.

End.

End.

Pebbles and Shells

DESIGNED BY DARA TOMASSON

Pebbles and Shells is a fantastic design that can be used as an allover dense fill. It's labor intensive if using as a detailed fill, so be aware of the time commitment. If done on a larger scale, the quilting can go quickly with stunning results. On the corner and square, stitch the shell or swirl (black lines) by creating an initial swirl, then use its base as a pivot point as you echo the circle with pebbles (blue lines) until you've filled the desired space. Alternate the size of the shells beside each other to help balance out the design. For the border, stitch the wavy row of pebbles first.

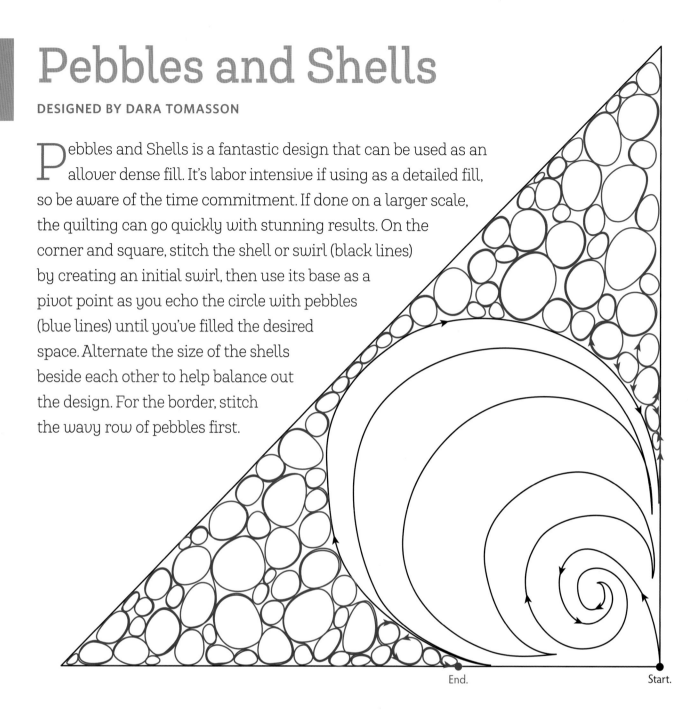

End.   Start.

Start.

Start.

End.

Fancy Clams

DESIGNED BY VICKI RUEBEL

Fancy Clams adds great texture to your quilt. Drawing reference lines will keep the clams similar in size. Each clam has three layers. Stitch the largest outside clam, then the middle clam, then the smallest clam. Travel along the bottom of the clam to start the next one. Half clams help fill the odd areas when quilting Fancy Clams in corners or squares. The design is great for both beginners and experienced quilters.

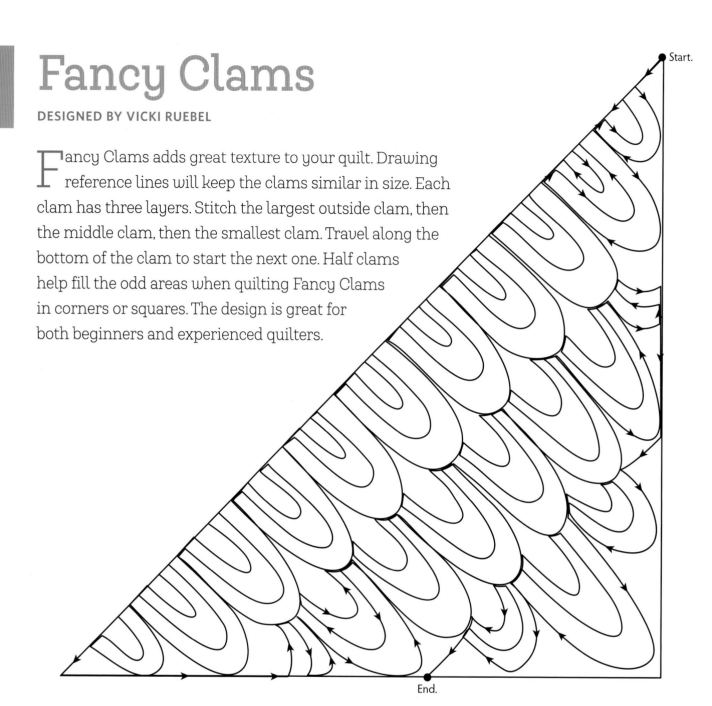

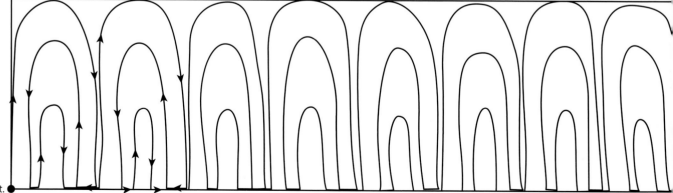

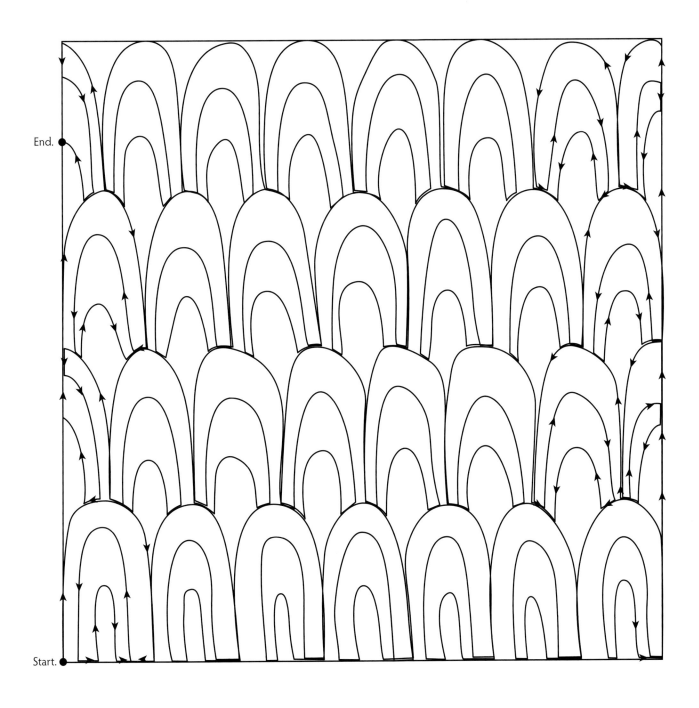

Start.

End.

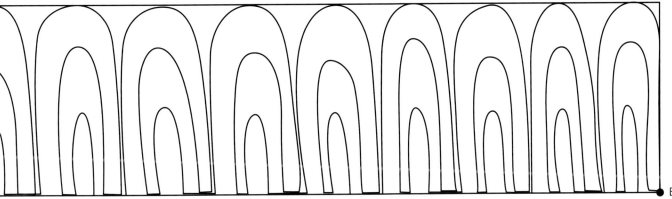

End.

Pumpkin Pearls

DESIGNED BY TRACEY BROWNING

Looking for an elegant design for a formal quilt? Stitch circles or ovals to create the smooth curves of the pumpkin seeds and fill with continuous pearls. The sashing or border design has two continuous passes easily created within equal divisions. Stitch the black path first, then end with the blue path. The block design uses continuous arcs that are then filled with pearls. Use this as a stand-alone motif, or fill the block background with curved crosshatching using the outer curves.

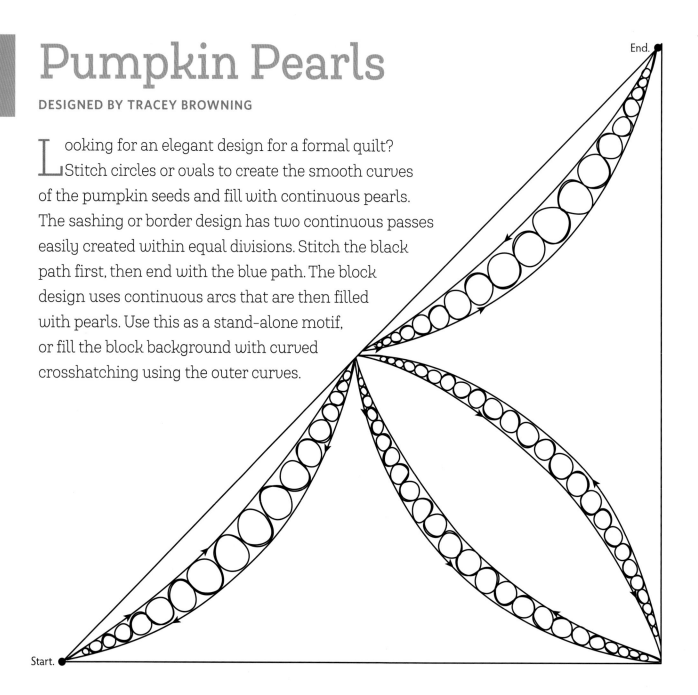

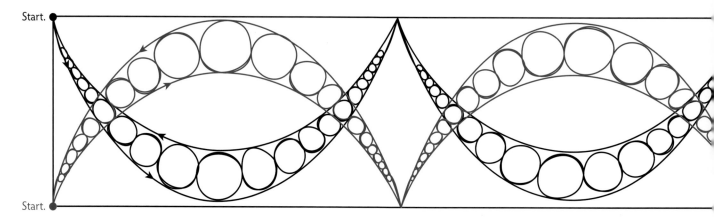

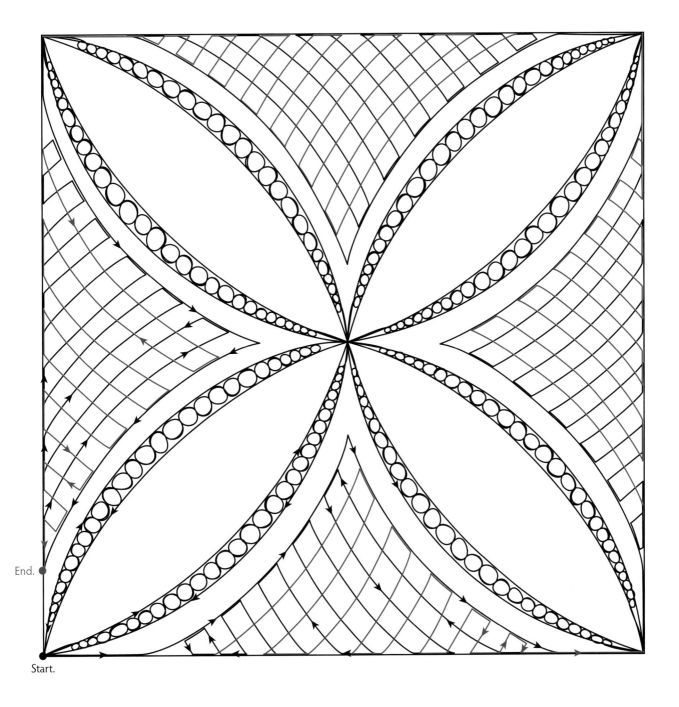

End.

Start.

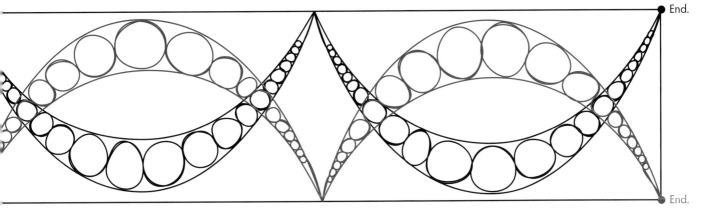

End.

End.

Oval Orange Peel

DESIGNED BY REBECCA SILBAUGH

Think of this design as the more outgoing cousin of the classic circular orange peel. It's quite similar and still has a traditional undertone, but it's more whimsical and playful. Oval Orange Peel is a great choice for those quilts that teeter on the line between modern and traditional—the quilting doesn't need to be the tiebreaker. Stitch the black path first (do half the oval going one way, and then half going the other way), followed by the blue path, and end by stitching the red path.

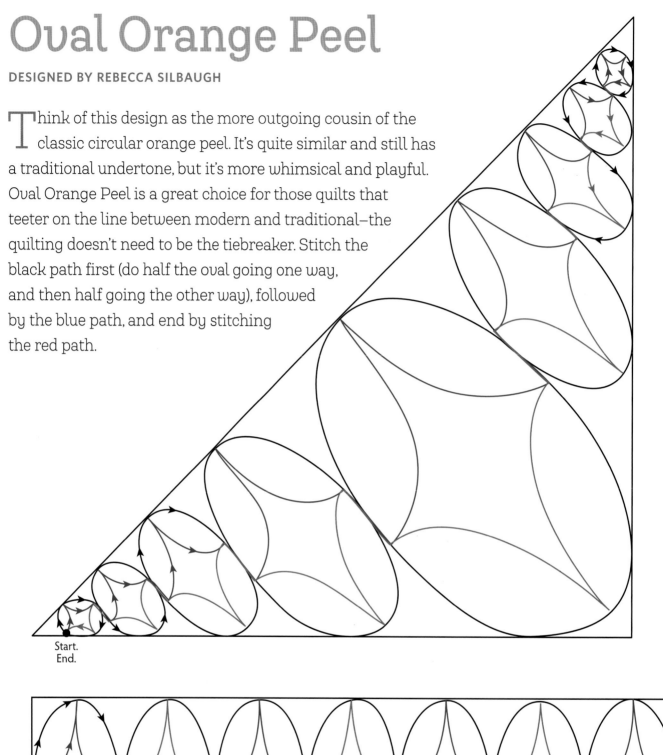

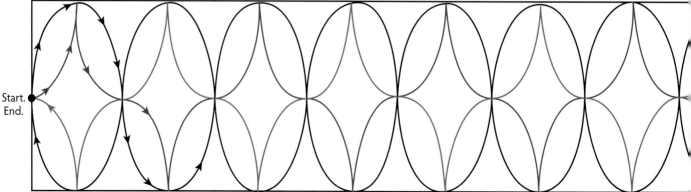

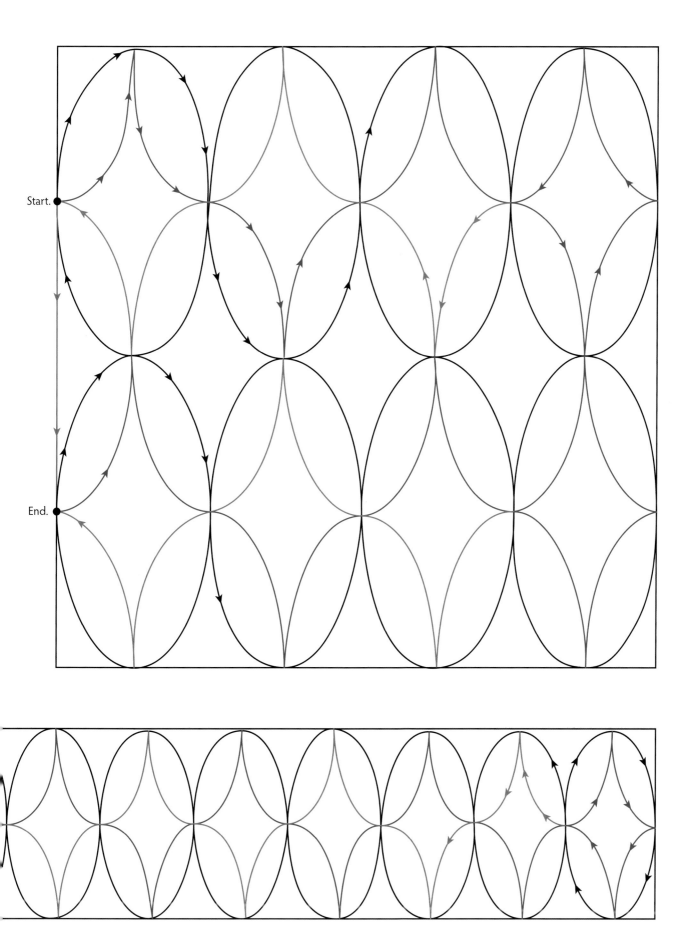

Start.

End.

Cross My Fingers

DESIGNED BY DARA TOMASSON

Since using straight lines to establish this design can be a bit intimidating, it's helpful to practice straight lines using a walking foot. Once you've established the lines with the walking foot, use the darning foot to finish with free-motion quilting. Cross My Fingers becomes more challenging the larger your scale, so beginners might want to practice on a small project. Start by stitching the black path, followed by the blue path, and end with the red path.

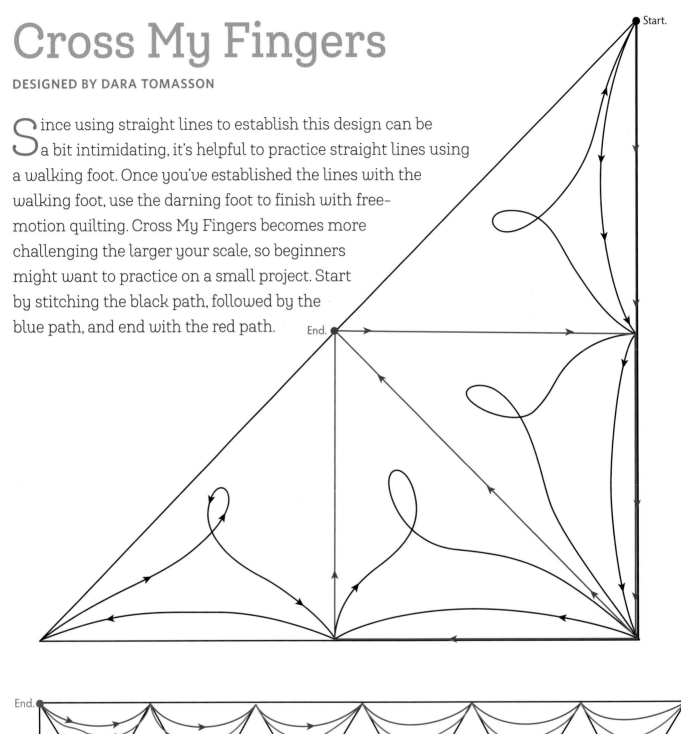

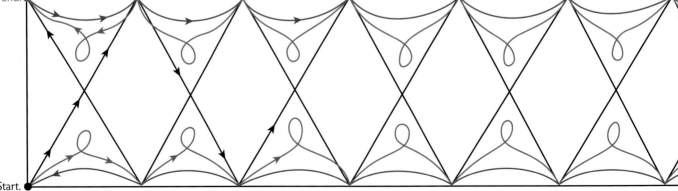

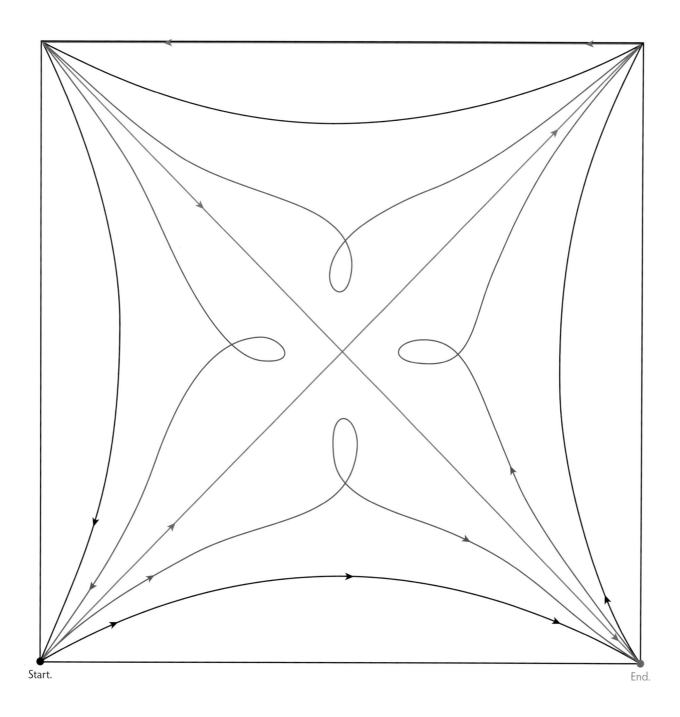

Start.

End.

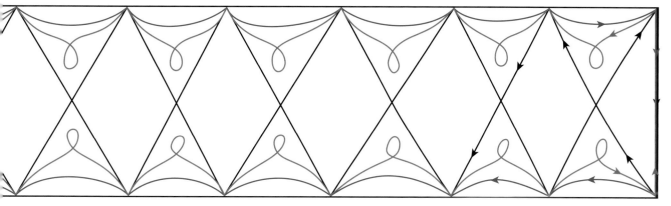

Beads

DESIGNED BY KAREN M. BURNS

A time-consuming design, Beads makes a great impact. Quilt the grid lines first; they can be as close together or as far apart as you wish. Then fill in with the round bead quilting. Row upon row of beads will really help define your all-important muscle memory and build your quilting confidence.

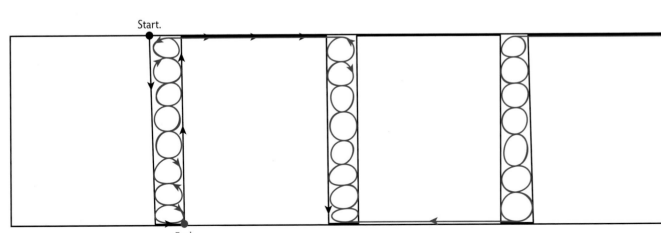

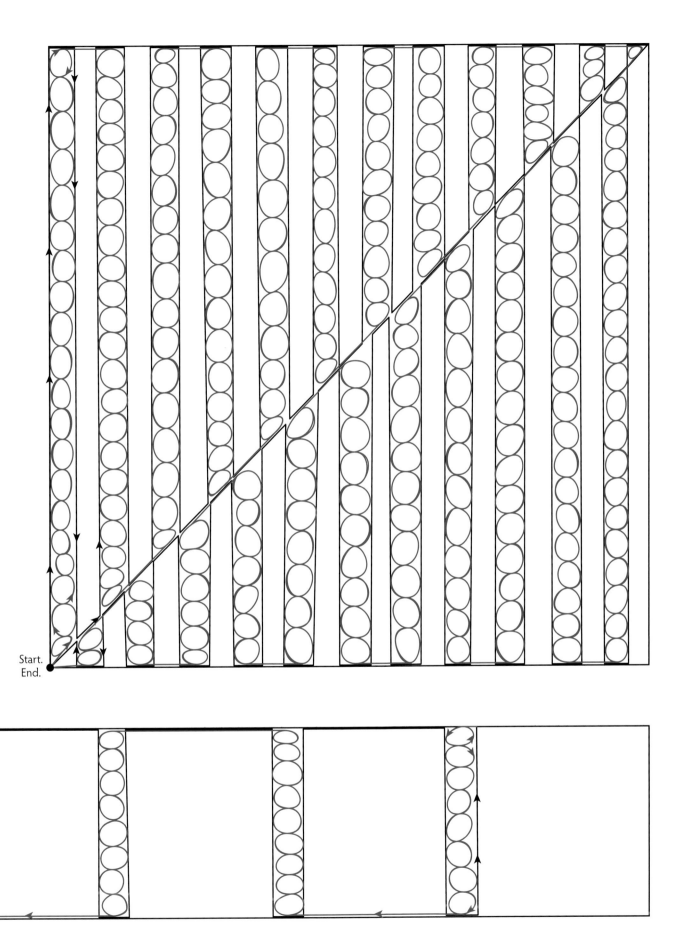

Start.
End.

Bright Idea

DESIGNED BY VICKI RUEBEL

Create a fun design by using a simple orange peel paired with a double loop. To execute this design, stitch the orange peels and fill in the double loops when you reach the corners. For the border application, travel along the seamline and randomly add the double loops. You can add more layers to the loops for extra pizazz. Measuring distance is not necessary.

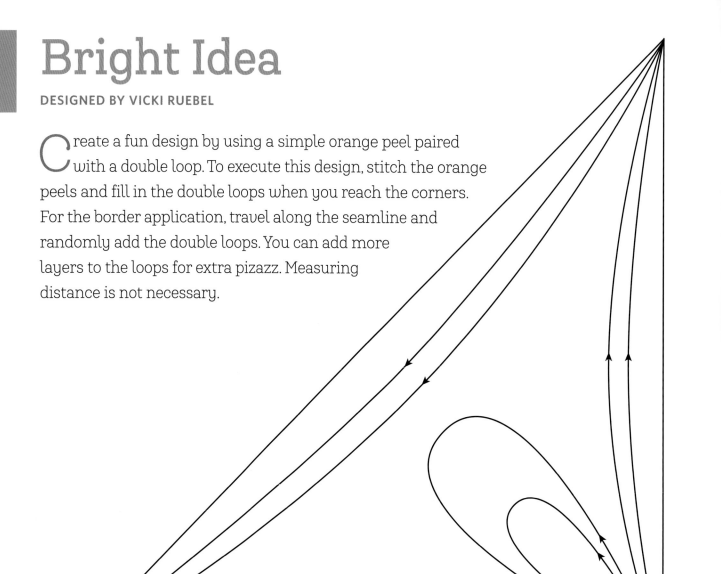

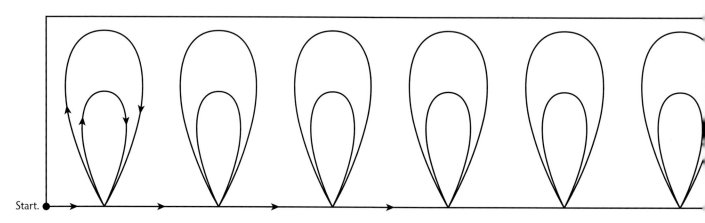

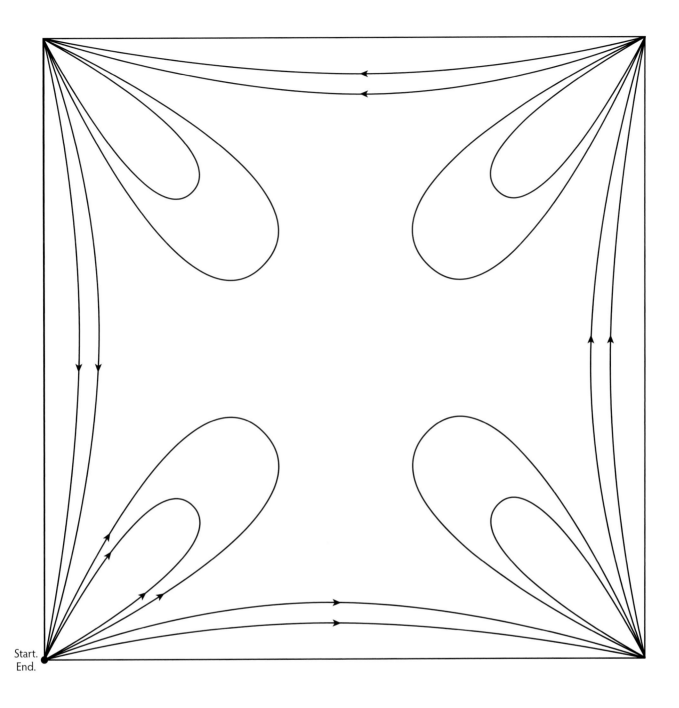

Start.
End.

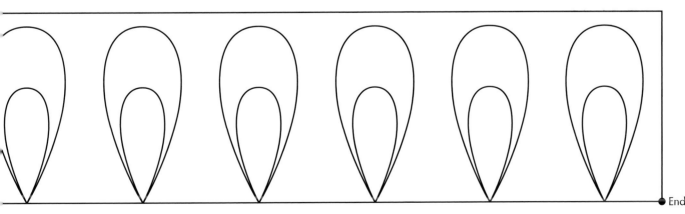

End.

Go Big or Go Home

DESIGNED BY REBECCA SILBAUGH

The name for this design comes from the little reminder Rebecca gives to herself as she's quilting. It's best to choose a direction to work (counterclockwise, for example) and always start with the big inward curve. By going the same direction and starting the same, the design will always match, whether you quilt it all at once or in sections (like a border or sashing). Begin with the black path and then finish by following the blue path.

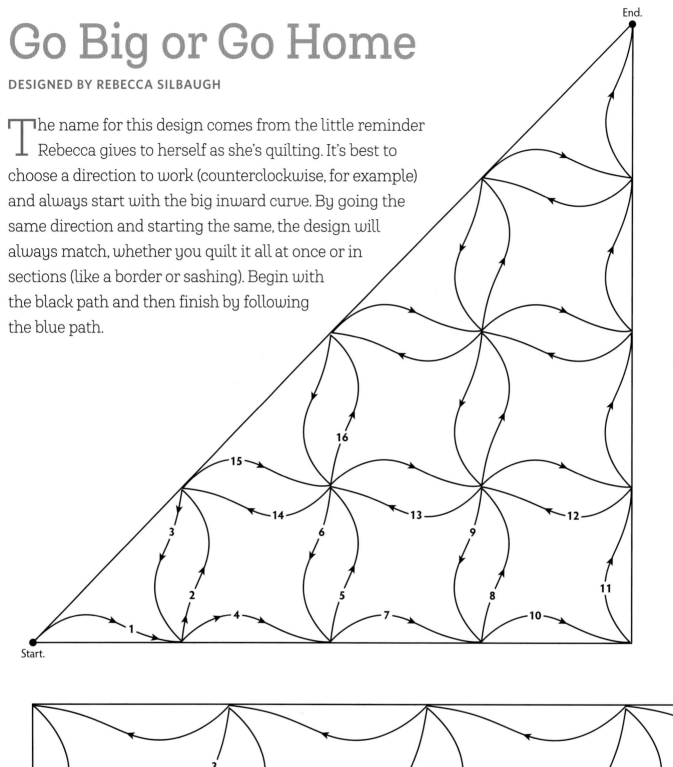

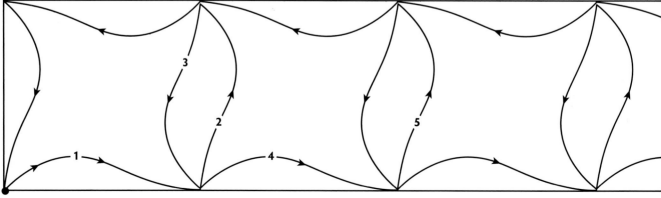

Start.
End.

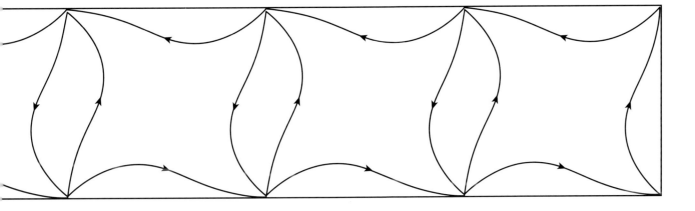

Fancy Keys

DESIGNED BY VICKI RUEBEL

Fancy Keys works great in any border size. Filling in random sections with ribbon candy adds texture and visual appeal to the design. Begin by stitching the straight lines and then choose where you will add the ribbon candy. You can stitch this design with the help of a ruler to create accurate straight lines or you can freehand the lines. Measuring the distance between the keys is not necessary. Make them random for a quick and easy design.

Start.

End.

Start.

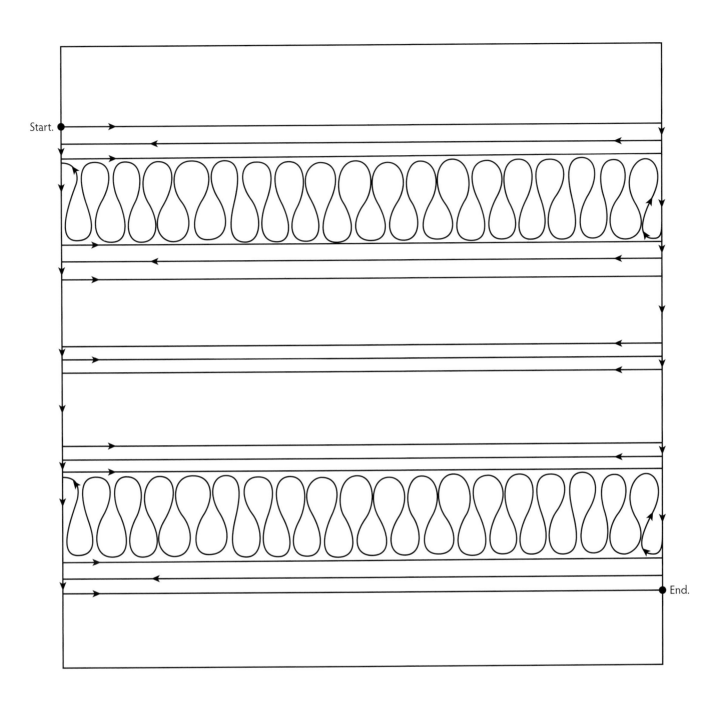

Start.

End.

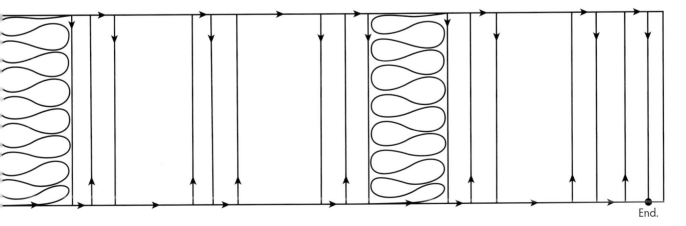

End.

Squiggle Dot

DESIGNED BY MAGGI HONEYMAN

Before quilting the long curved lines, use an acrylic ruler to establish the square and triangle of Squiggle Dot. Continue without stopping to create the dots next, and you should end up back at the starting place. The squiggle lines come last. For the border, chalk the lines for the "blocks," then start at the beginning of the border and quilt the squiggle lines continuously.

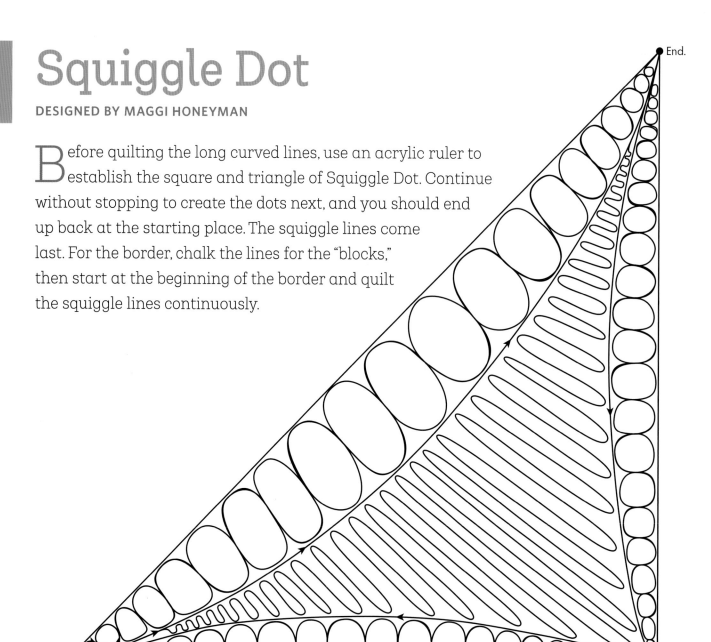

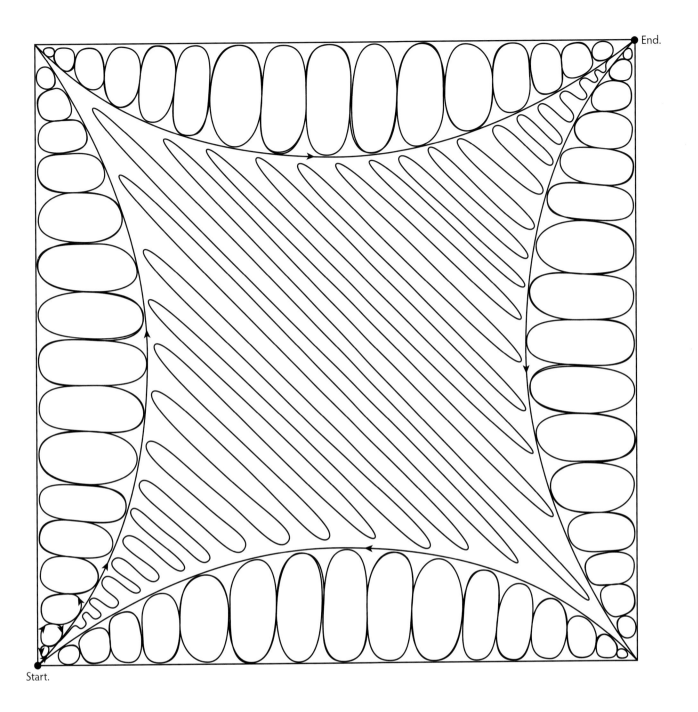

End.

Start.

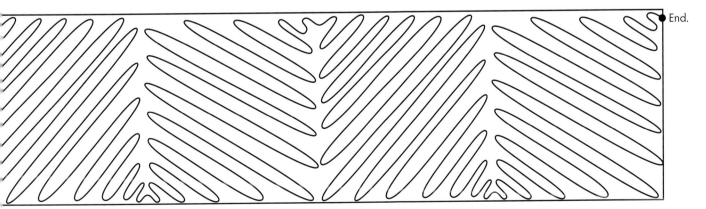

End.

Butterfly Feathers

DESIGNED BY KRYSTAL JAKELWICZ

Butterfly Feathers makes a lovely echoing feather. Start by creating a smaller base petal first (black lines) and echoing twice (blue and red lines) to fill in the block's space. Travel back down the feather and repeat. Then just bounce the small feathers off the base feather echo at the top and make your way back down to finish off the petal. For the border, start by creating a base center feather with echoing petals to fill in. Fill in with more butterfly feathers. Then curve a "scallop" to the second point and echo back and forth.

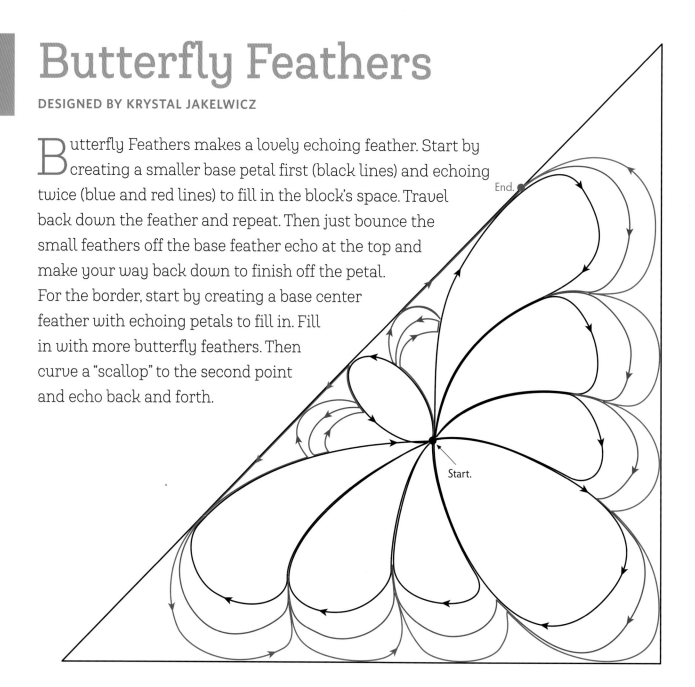

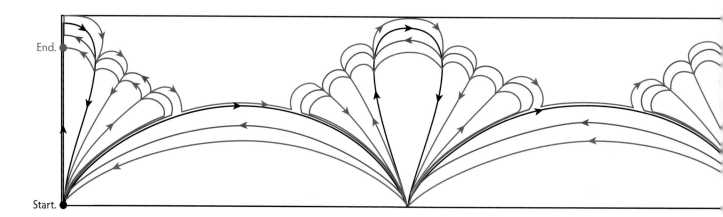

End.

Start.

Pineapple Craze

DESIGNED BY KELSI KARG

These swirls and curves have the bonus of a pineapple motif, which lends a fruity sweet finish to a table topper, runner, or kitchen wall hanging! Crisscross over the pineapples as shown or leave them open for a silhouette effect. To achieve the symmetry in this design, it's best to draw in the pineapples and tops with an erasable ink pen. Then, if you have mad doodling skills, start doodling—or cheat a little and ink in the entire design before you stitch. Work the black lines first, followed by the blue lines.

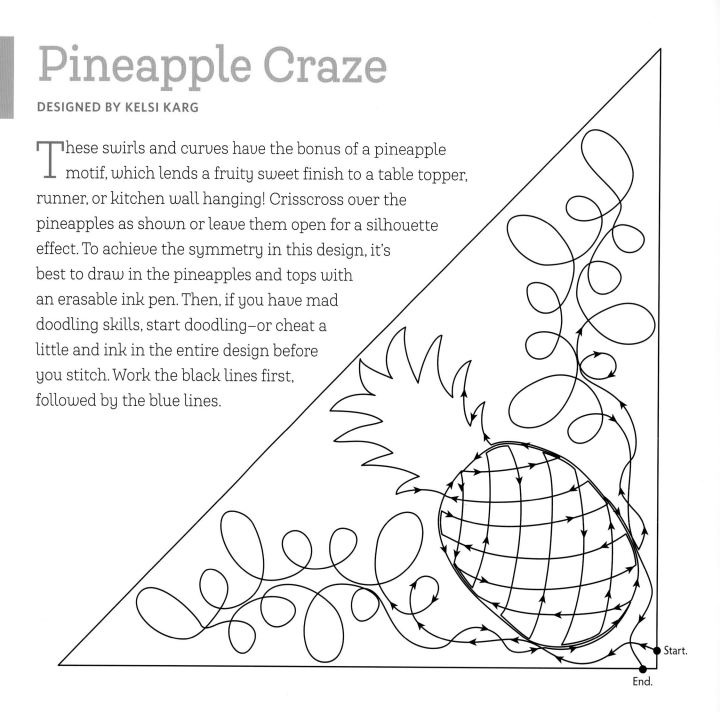

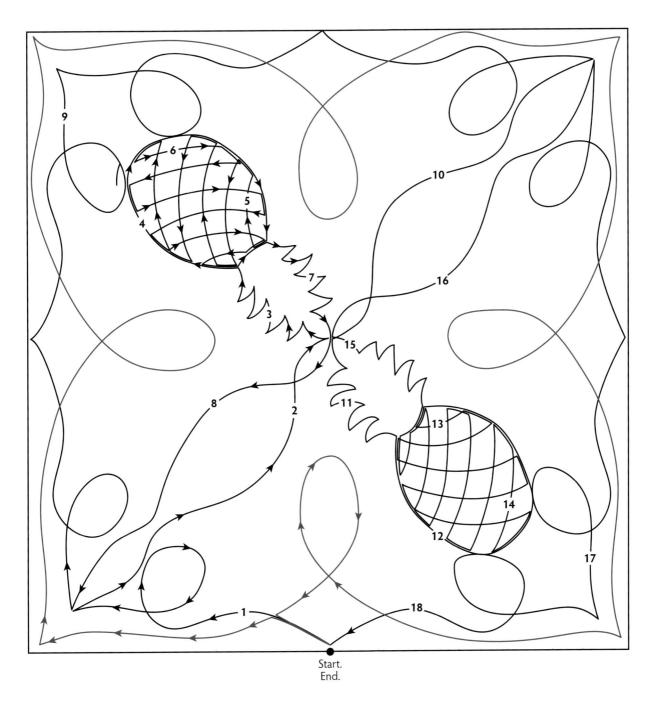

Start.
End.

End.

End.

Leaves and Qs

DESIGNED BY KAREN M. BURNS

Leaves and Qs gives a nod to nature, meandering in an allover fill just like live vines. It's easy to add as many leaves and spirals as you need in this design, which gives you the freedom to fill any shape or space. The corner design directs the path in a slight curve, the border is a single straight path, and the block design travels up and down, filling the square. If you need to cover a larger space, simply enlarge the elements.

End.

Start.

Start.

Start.

End.

End.

Mighty Oak

DESIGNED BY DARA TOMASSON

Autumn, with its richly colored leaves, was this pattern's inspiration. Mighty Oak is a fabulous quilting design to enhance autumn quilts, table runners, and other seasonal projects. For this design, each leaf is created differently. Curlicues are stitched at the base of each leaf to add variety, and you can bend the vine or change the leaf size to fill the desired space. When creating this design, stitch the center spine, trace it back on itself, and continue to the leaf design from the spine.

Start.
End.

Start.

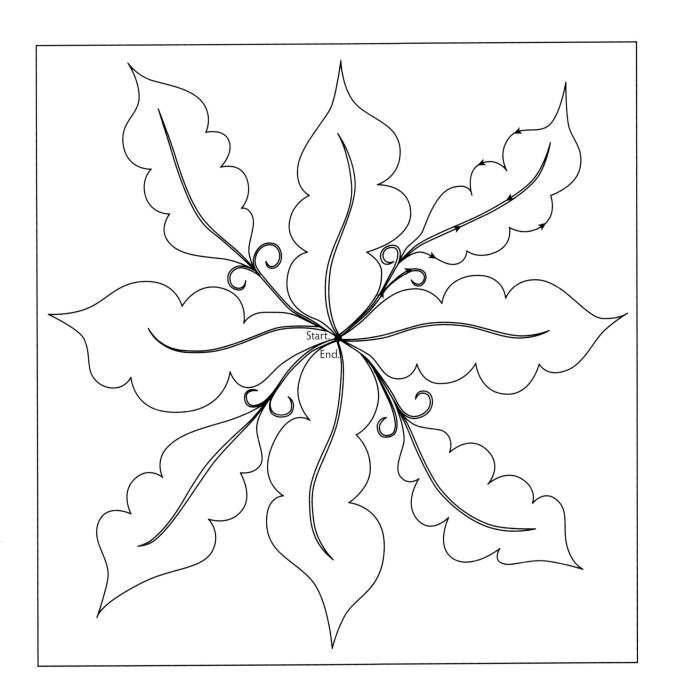

Start.
End.

End.

Curling Leaves

DESIGNED BY LAURIE GUSTAFSON

Curling Leaves is a playfully romantic feather-and-swirl design. It's great for traditionally pieced quilts with a botanical feel. Start with the outer arc of each feather and then gradually make smaller leaves curling inward. Think of a fern unfurling. Finally, add a few random curls to fill in remaining blank spaces.

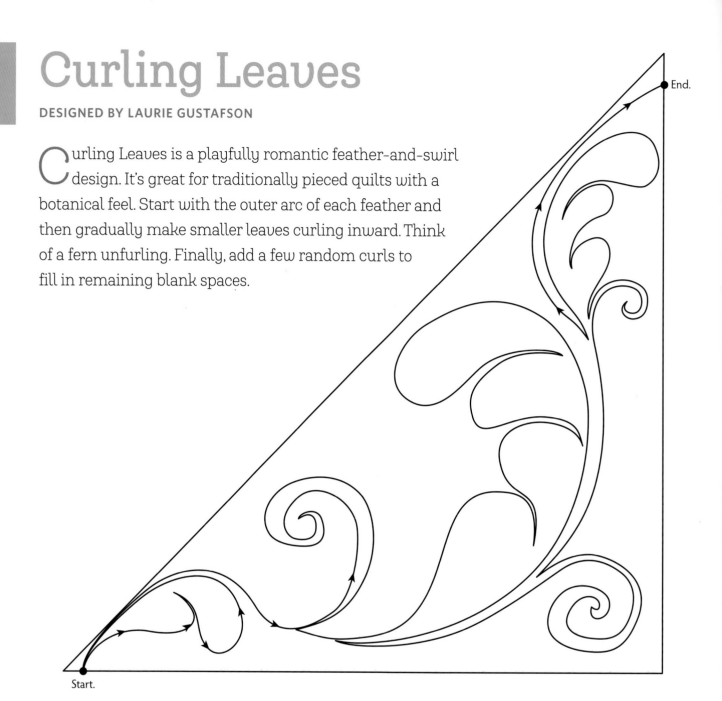

Start.

End.

Start.

Start.

End.

End.

Hooked Paisley

DESIGNED BY TRACEY BROWNING

The Hooked Paisley is a fast, free-flowing, and forgiving design. Simply start with a loop and echo it back like a hook, and then swap to the opposite side in the direction you wish to go. Chalk an eight-line grid on your block first, and then fill in the block design with echoed loops and feather hooks. Hooked Paisley looks fantastic in variegated threads for bold impact.

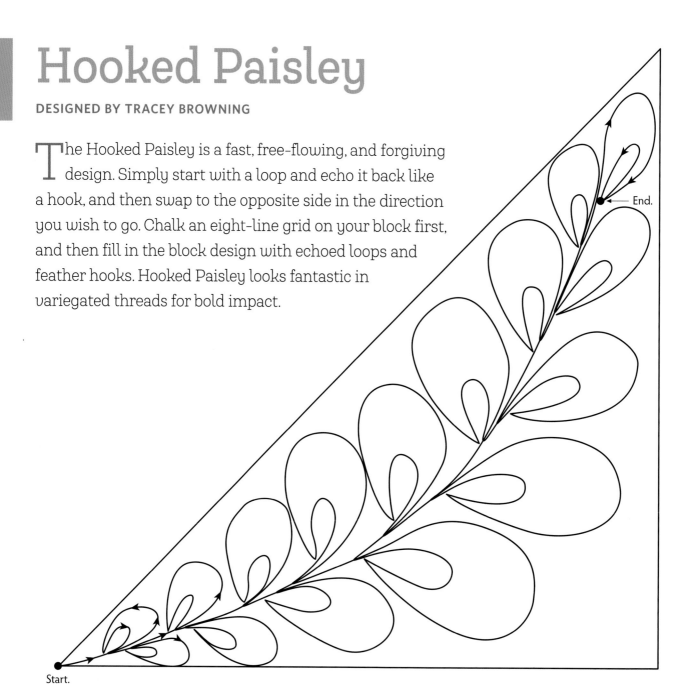

Start.
End.

End.

Fanfare

DESIGNED BY MAGGI HONEYMAN

Fanfare can start one of two ways. First, you could chalk in the diagonal lines, quilt the fan motifs, and then come back around to stitch over the chalked lines. Or, you could work the diagonals and zigzags first, and then fill in with the fans. Either way, you'll be making use of the ditches, stopping at the center point of each fan, quilting the center plume, and then visually dividing each half to finish the plumes on either side of the center.

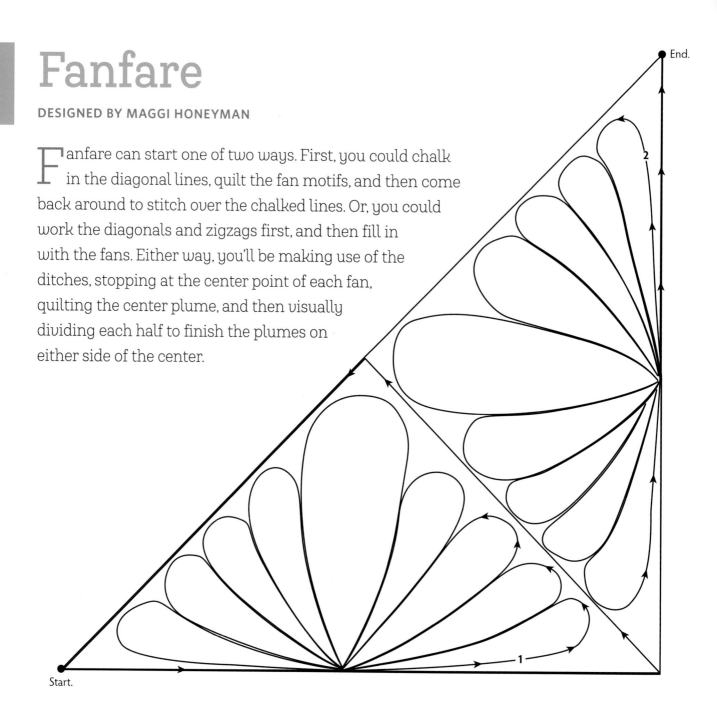

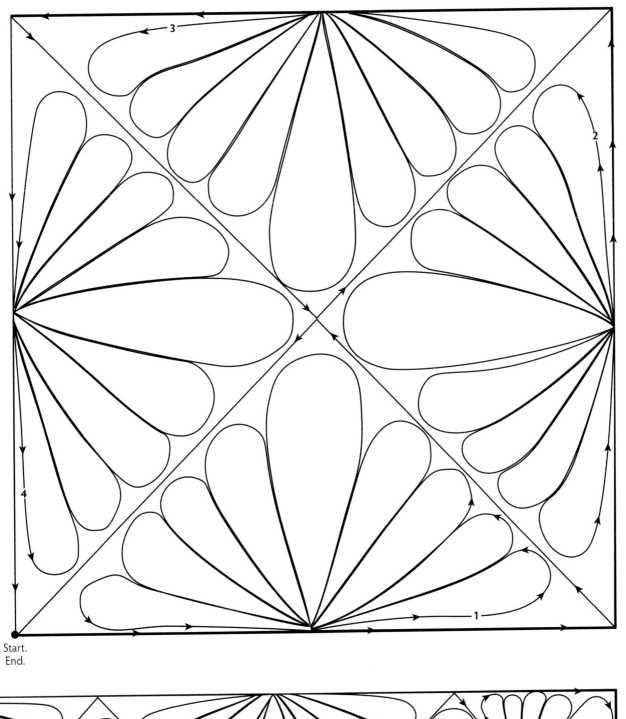

Start.
End.

End.

Floral Lines

DESIGNED BY KRYSTAL JAKELWICZ

Floral Lines is a beginner quilting design that helps you learn echoing. For the square block, start with large petals (black lines) that extend to the corners, then add a smaller echo petal (blue lines) within each one. In all versions, accent with petals that loop into pebbles on both sides (red lines) before ending back at the center. For the border, start from the left side, looping three petals. Then travel down the ditch of one petal to the next grouping of three. Add circular pebbles to the center or side petals as you see fit. You might want to use a marking tool to mark guides for the points.

Start. End.

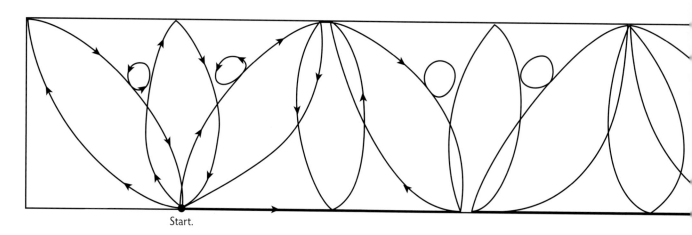

Start.

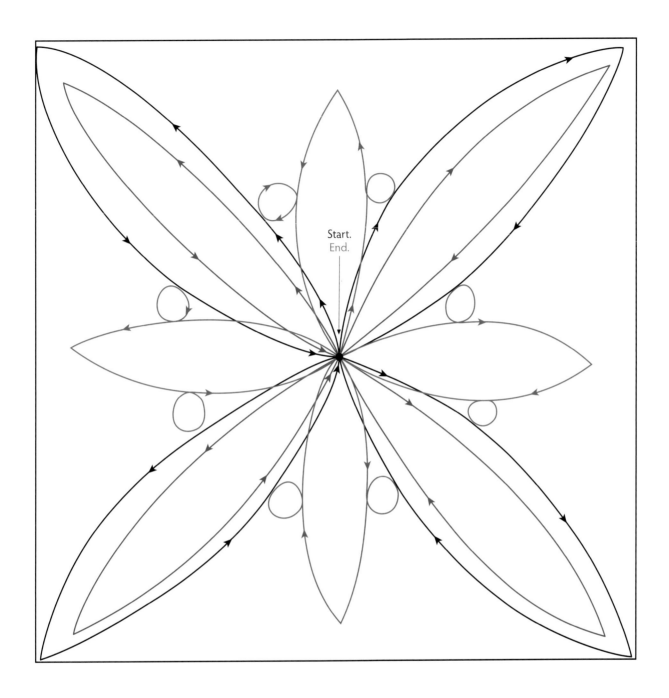

Start.
End.

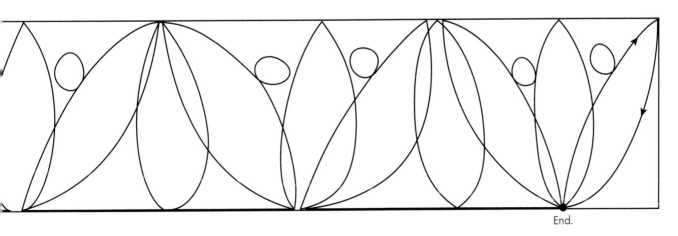

End.

Chocolate Vine

DESIGNED BY LORI KENNEDY

Need an easy replacement for traditional quilted feathers? Add a little chocolate to your quilt! The Chocolate Vine can bend and twist to fit myriad shapes. Begin by marking a wavy line to create the central stem of the design. Stitch the top row of leaves by stitching a loop, reversing direction to add an interior loop, then stitching along the drawn stem line to begin the next leaf. At the end of the stem line, add a leaf to form the tip, then begin stitching the lower set of leaves.

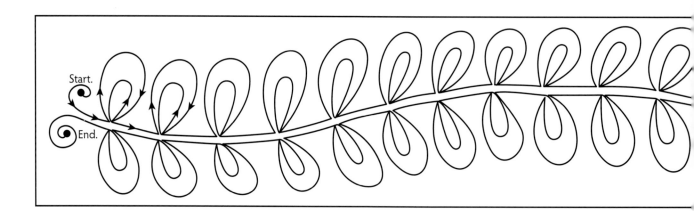

End.

Start.

End.

Start.

Searing Sun

DESIGNED BY LAURIE GUSTAFSON

If you live in a cloudy climate, you find yourself creating your own sunshine many days of the year. The Searing Sun design is easy to stitch; it's a center spiral with flames emanating outward. Don't worry if your lines cross; that's just part of this design's charm.

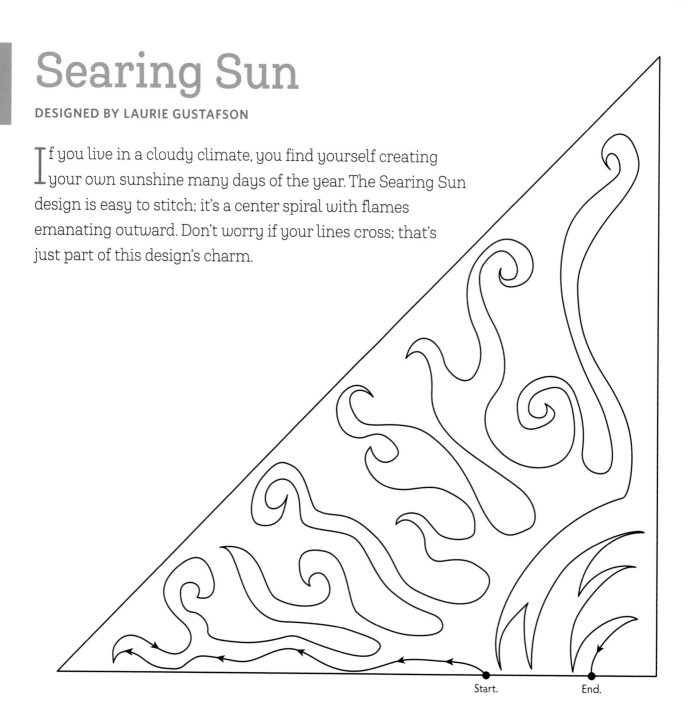

Start.

End.

Start.

Start.

End.

End.

Ivy

DESIGNED BY CAROLYN MURFITT

Ivy is a simple meandering design that adds leaves to curves, creating a lovely flowing vine. When quilting the leaf motif, always start with the vein line in the middle of the leaf, and then continue around the leaf shape. Use a Florentine curve—echoing the curve rather than stitching back over it—for an open, delicate finish.

Start.
End.

End.

Flame

DESIGNED BY KAREN M. BURNS

The Flame design lends dramatic movement to any quilt top. It fills the space quickly, and it looks nice in wide open spaces or as an allover design. Have fun with the flame shapes and don't overthink it. Start with a curl, and then add some pointy flames. You'll soon include this in your "go-to" design file.

Start.   End.

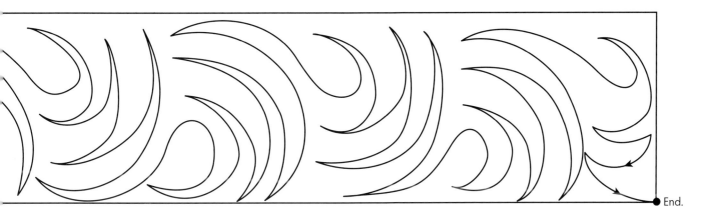

End.

Calla Lily

DESIGNED BY CAROLYN MURFITT

Calla Lily takes a meandering vine to the next level by adding simple flower shapes along the path. It's a sweet quilting pattern that looks much more difficult than it is. The only thing to remember, other than following the design line, is to quilt the stamen in the calla lily first, up and down, before continuing around the shape of the lily. To add fullness to your curves, separate the lines rather than doubling back over them.

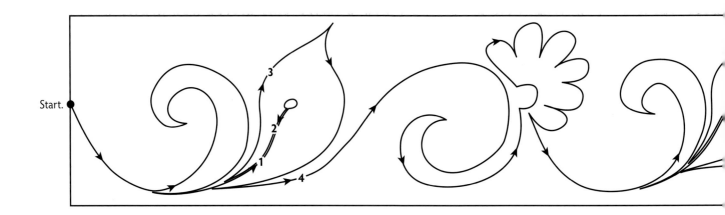

Start.
End.

End.

Loopy Daisies

DESIGNED BY MELISSA CORRY

Loopy Daisies is a fun free-motion design that will take you back to your days of childhood doodling. Start with some free-motion loops and then when you're ready to make a daisy, stitch a complete circle and double over the circle to where you plan to exit the flower. Work five petals counterclockwise around the circle. Exit and continue the loopy line.

End.

Start.

Start.

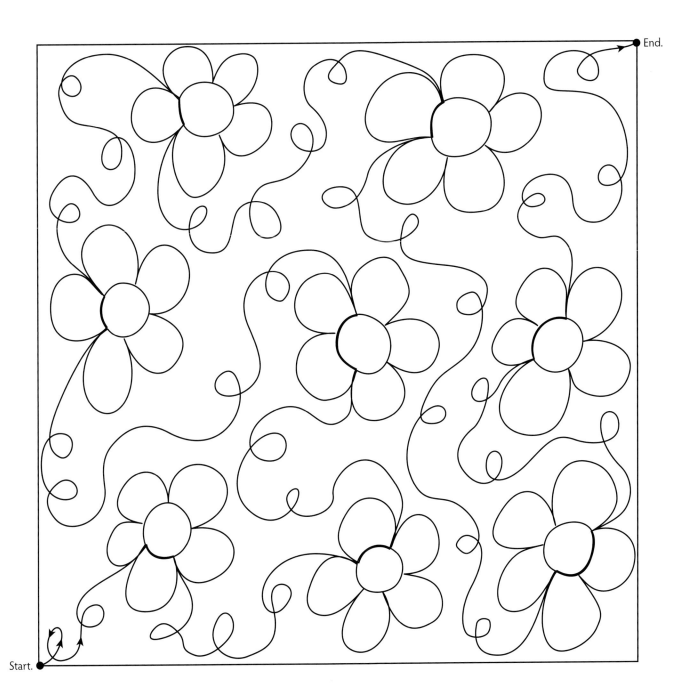

End.

Start.

End.

Roses

DESIGNED BY LAURIE GUSTAFSON

The Roses design is perfect to use with high-loft batting; the swirly, curvy lines make the batting puff up so beautifully it almost gives the flowers an overlapping effect. The design is simple and fun, starting with a swirl to create the center of the flower and then continuing with curvy lines around the centers of the roses. Each additional rose starts again with a swirl, but the curvy lines help you to nestle the roses between each other.

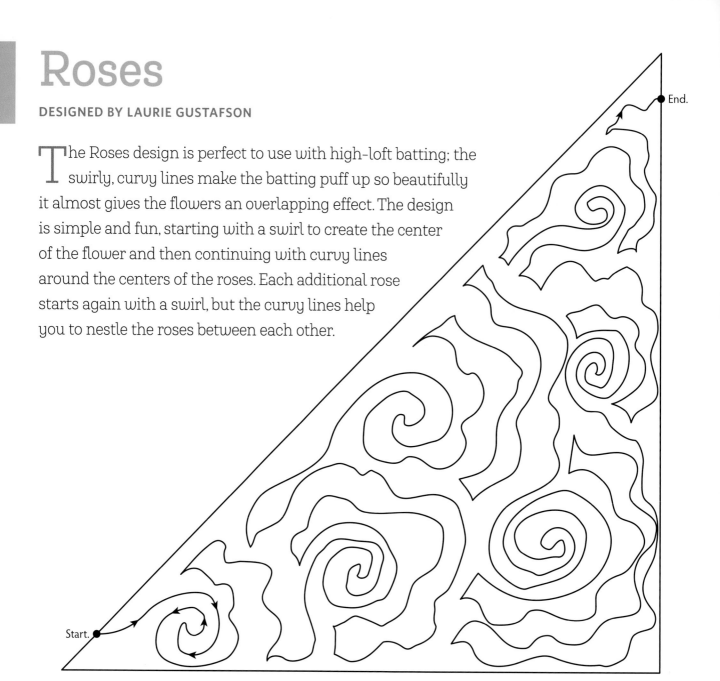

Start.

End.

End.

Nancy's Rose

DESIGNED BY LORI KENNEDY

An elegant spiral rose, this motif is named for the late Nancy Zieman, of *Sewing with Nancy* fame, who loved it. No need to be neat as you stitch a clockwise spiral from the outer border to the center and back out again. Add a leaf and echo stitch the interior of the leaf, adding a center vein line before beginning the next leaf around the central rose. Stitch swirls between each leaf to fill the square block. For more variety, add a cluster of small roses in place of the large rose in the square block.

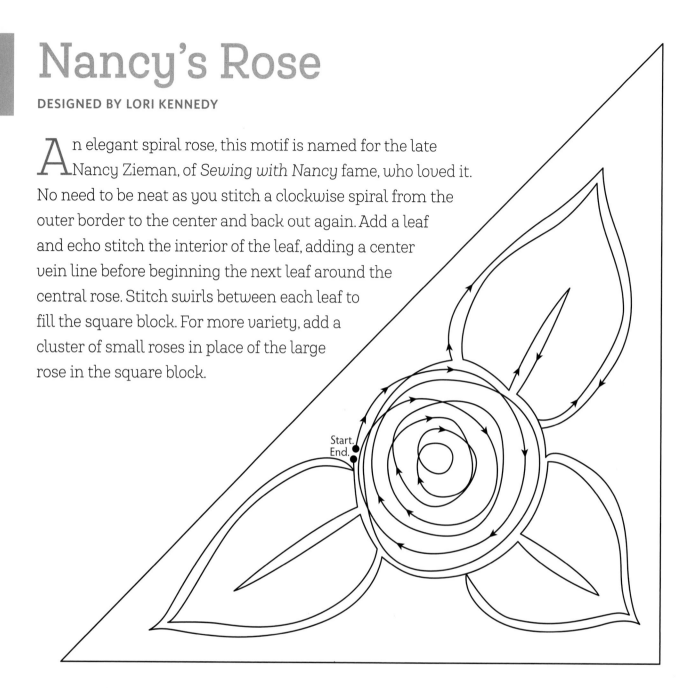

Sunflower

DESIGNED BY MAGGI HONEYMAN

Stitch around an acrylic circle template to achieve the perfect center for each sunflower. After the circle is established, fill in the center with the pebbles, stopping back at the point where you started the circle. Without breaking thread, stitch the petals just as you would a feathered wreath, ending at the original starting point.

Start.
End.

Start.

Start.
End.

End.

Strawflower

DESIGNED BY DIXIE THUE

This is a fast and fun design. Start in the center and work outward until you're happy with the number of petals. You can make this flower as large or small as you like. For the border, divide the space into equal parts before you begin and then create each flower as described above. Traveling to the next flower simply adds more texture to your border. You can try the same idea to fill in small Strawflowers in the corners of a large setting triangle too.

Start.
End.

Start.

Start.
End.

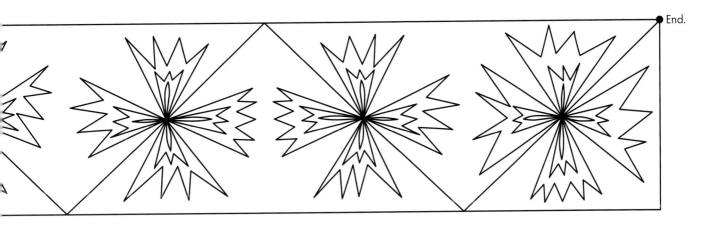

End.

Traditional Sunflower

DESIGNED BY KRYSTAL JAKELWICZ

Traditional Sunflower is a striking option for floral quilts. For the corner and border designs, start by drawing a partial circle, then quilt the larger base petals every 45° around the circle. Once you've completed the base petals, travel along the tips of those petals, adding background petal tips between the base petals. This will help give your petals some detail.

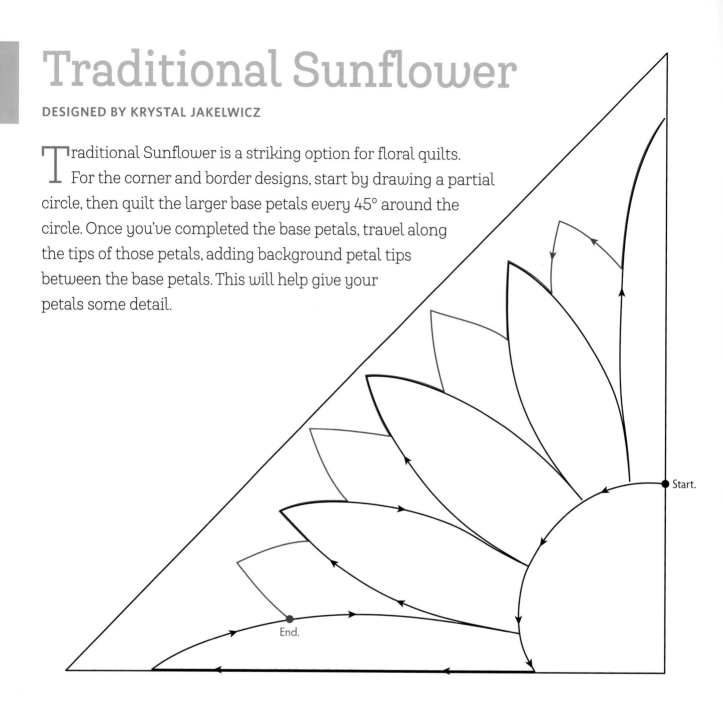

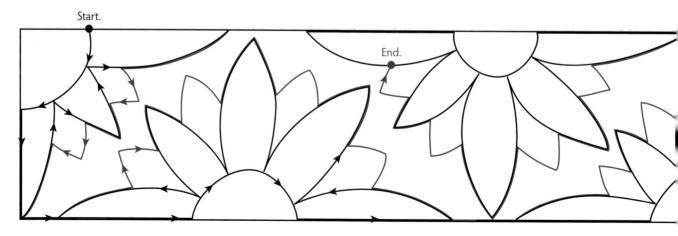

Start.

End.

Flower Power

DESIGNED BY KAREN M. BURNS

A mod, allover floral vine with a '70s hippie charm, Flower Power incorporates loops, spirals, and a feathery petal. Vary the size and shape of the flowers and spirals to fill the space. Some echo quilting around the flower petals adds additional filler and is used as a connection point.

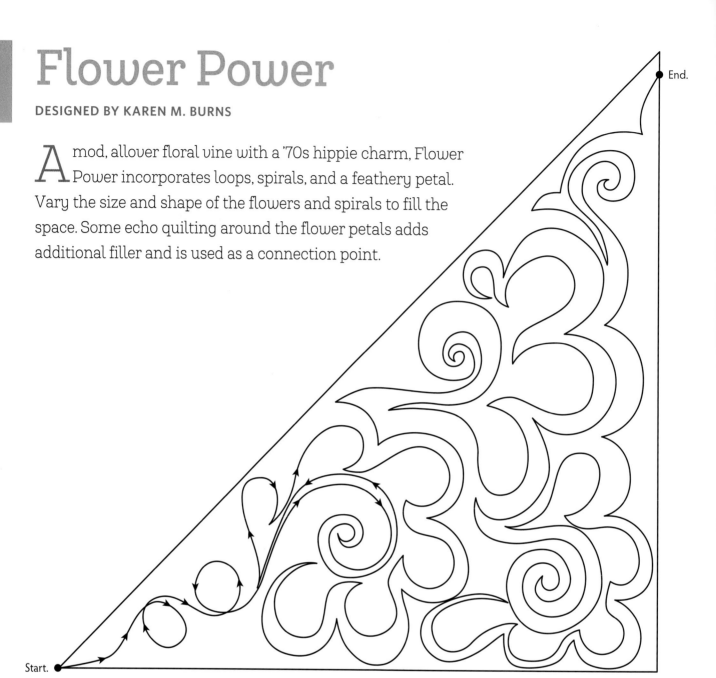

End.
Start.

End.

Dandelions

DESIGNED BY KARRLYN MARCHUK

The Dandelions motif is fun and lively. Before getting started, mark the quilting space with a ruler and fabric pen as a guide for the dandelion head placement. Start by outlining the leaves and continuing to the stem. For the head of the dandelion, use straight lines, stitching back and forth to create texture. To avoid thread buildup, echo back along each straight line rather than stitching directly on it. This will give the extra benefit of fluffing out each dandelion.

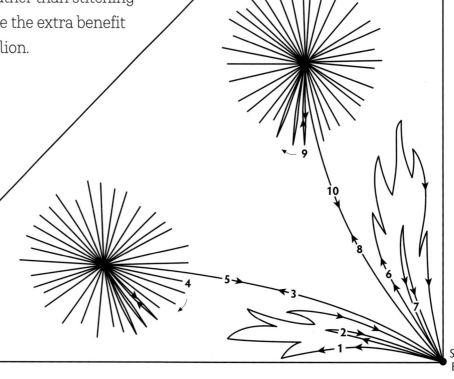

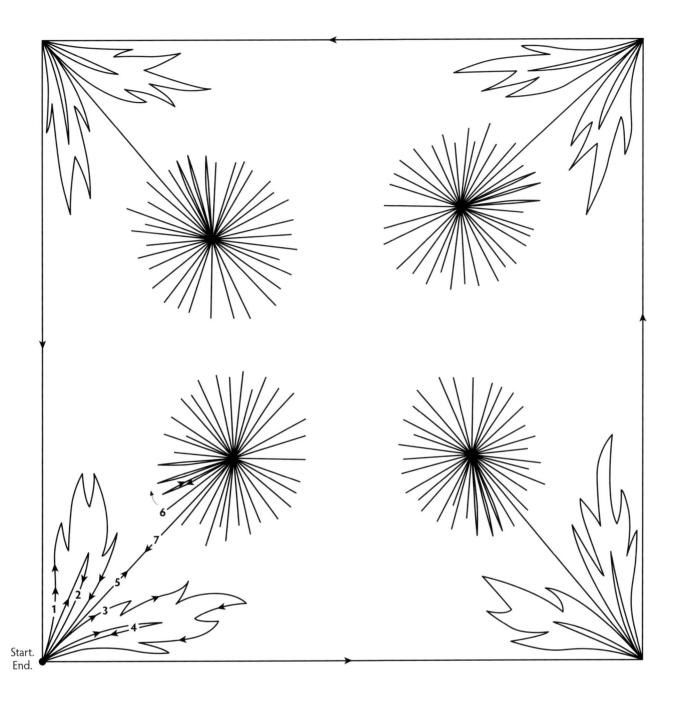

Start.
End.

End.

Daisy to Be Square

DESIGNED BY DARA TOMASSON

Change the shape of a familiar design to freshen up your quilting. Try to be precise when meeting your stitches at the center on these triangle daisies. Practice on paper first! On the first pass of the border design, stitch evenly spaced vertical lines, then use the lines to stitch equally spaced diamonds, alternating with small triangles. Echo back with smaller diamonds. The square design is a meandering line interspersed with daisies. The corner is filled with evenly spaced daisies along an angled line.

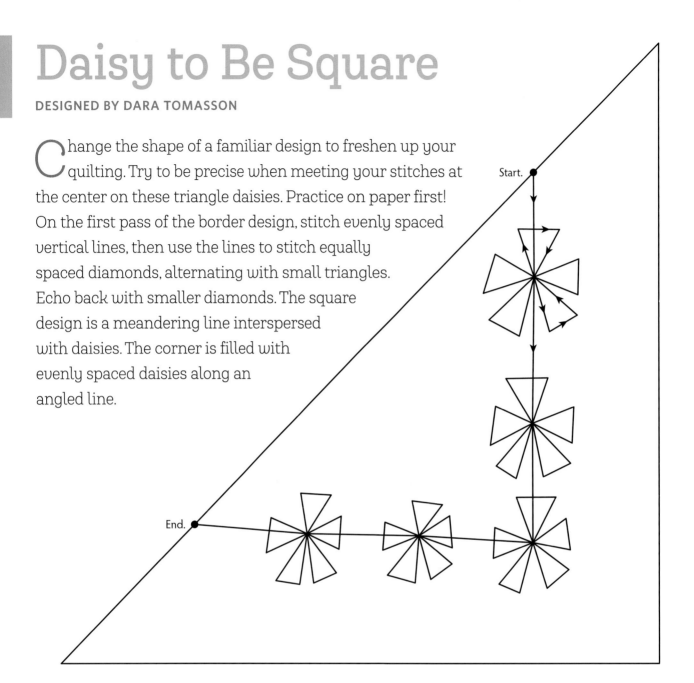

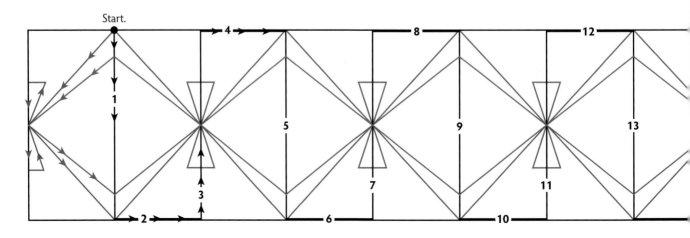

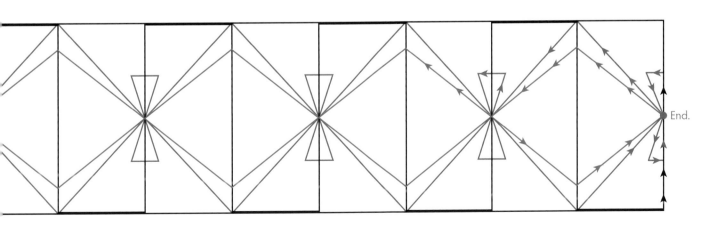

End.

Mason Jar Love

DESIGNED BY KELSI KARG

Mason Jar is pebble quilting with lots of novelty twists—hearts, mason jars, and a dash of love. The border design has two passes: the first is a row of loopy hearts and the second is pebbles that continue right into the mason jars. The bases and tops on all the jars are essentially wide, flat pebbles. You can stitch the corner design however you prefer. Begin with pebbles or create the jar first and use pebbles to travel to the next jar.

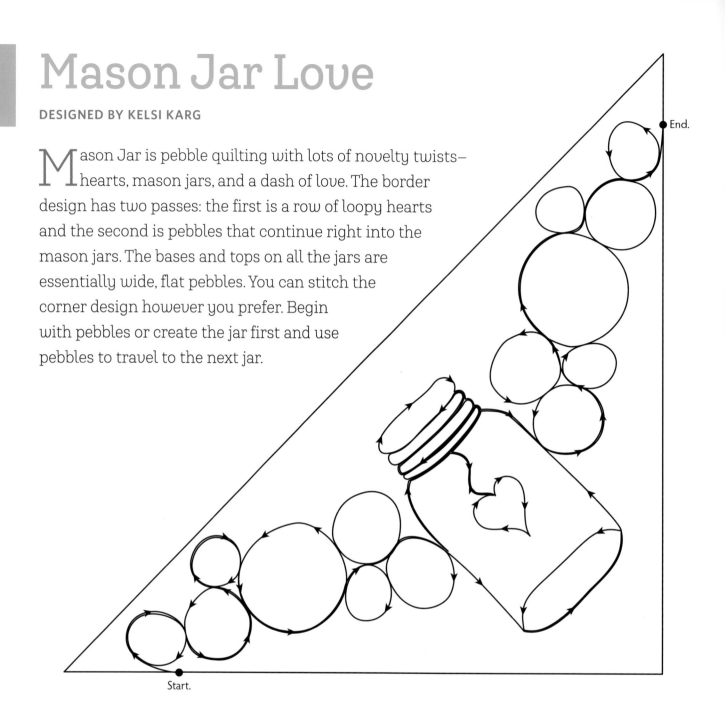

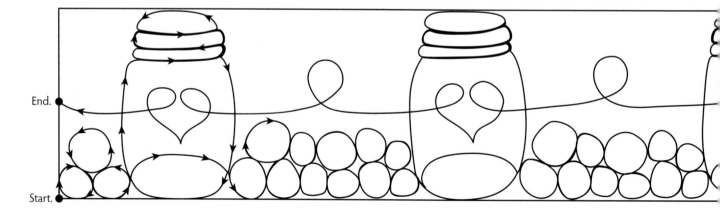

Start.

Love

End.

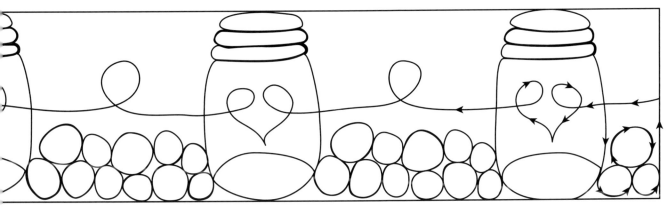

Tree-Lined Street

DESIGNED BY LORI KENNEDY

Add a touch of home sweet home to your quilts with a charming row of houses. Stitch the left side of each house, jog to the left and stitch a triangle roof, and then complete the house with a simple rectangle door. Add circles for bushes and trees to complete your quilted Tree-Lined Street. For more variety, change the roof shape or add chimneys, windows, stairs, and other details to your houses.

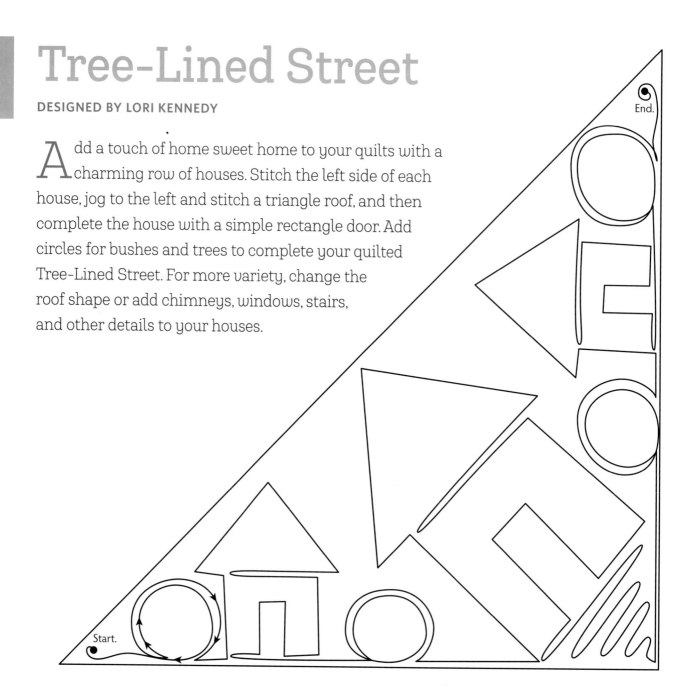

Start.

End.

End.

Spider Power

DESIGNED BY DARA TOMASSON

Spider Power requires a fair bit of tracing back on itself. This design requires dividing up the space with lines, but remember, spiderwebs are organic and natural. Use a ruler and fabric pen to measure and mark midpoints on the square so that the framework is fairly symmetrical. After creating the X and then the dissection, retrace back to the center and create the webs using curved lines that spiral out and echo each other. On the border, the spiders connect the boxed webs.

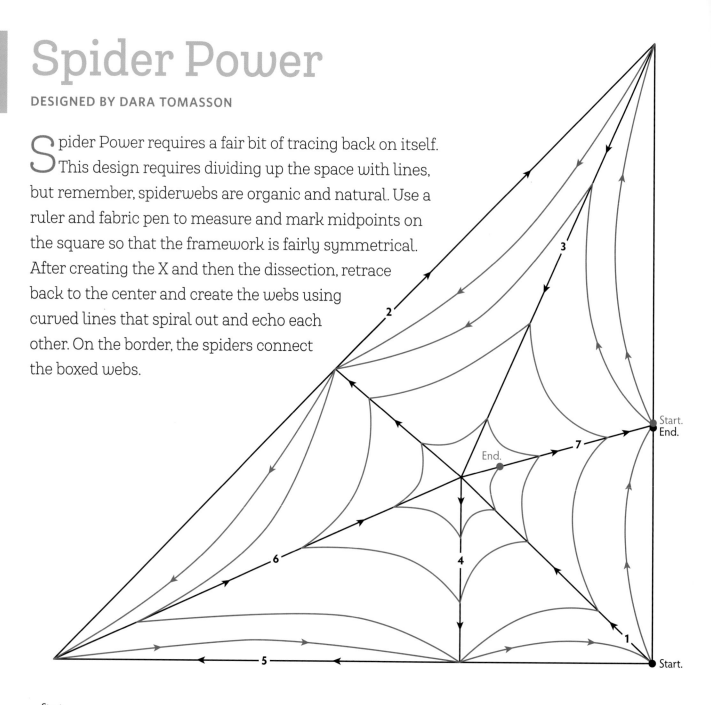

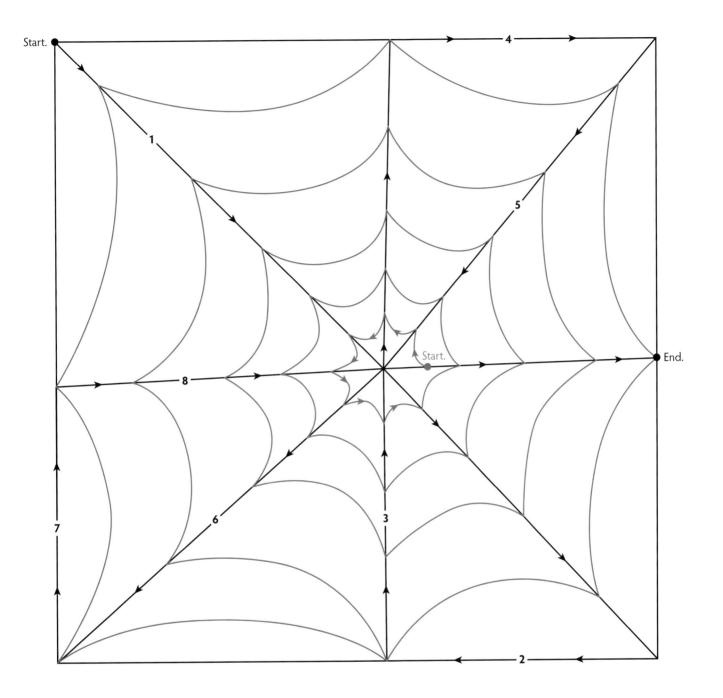

Start.

4

1

5

Start.

End.

8

7

6

3

2

End.

End.

Spiderweb Herringbone

DESIGNED BY REBECCA SILBAUGH

A chevron feel with the novelty of a web, Spiderweb Herringbone is a perfect complement to Spider Power on page 106. Whether you quilt your guides or stitch-in-the-ditch of your quilt, the guides lay the foundation. After that, move up and down as you work from side to side and echo the curves. You're striving for fun with this design, so relax and enjoy. Work the black paths first and end with the blue paths.

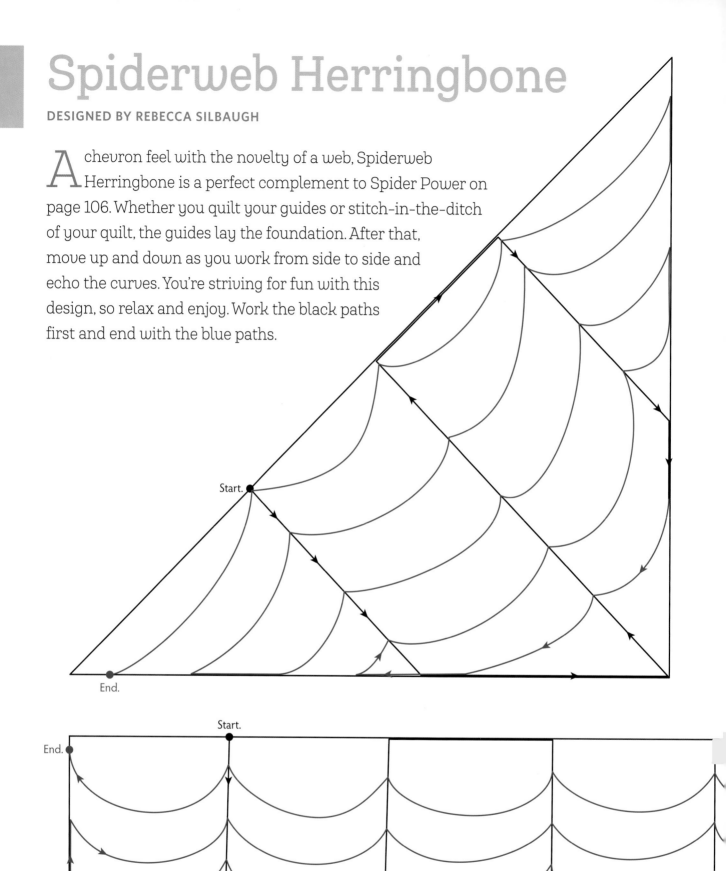

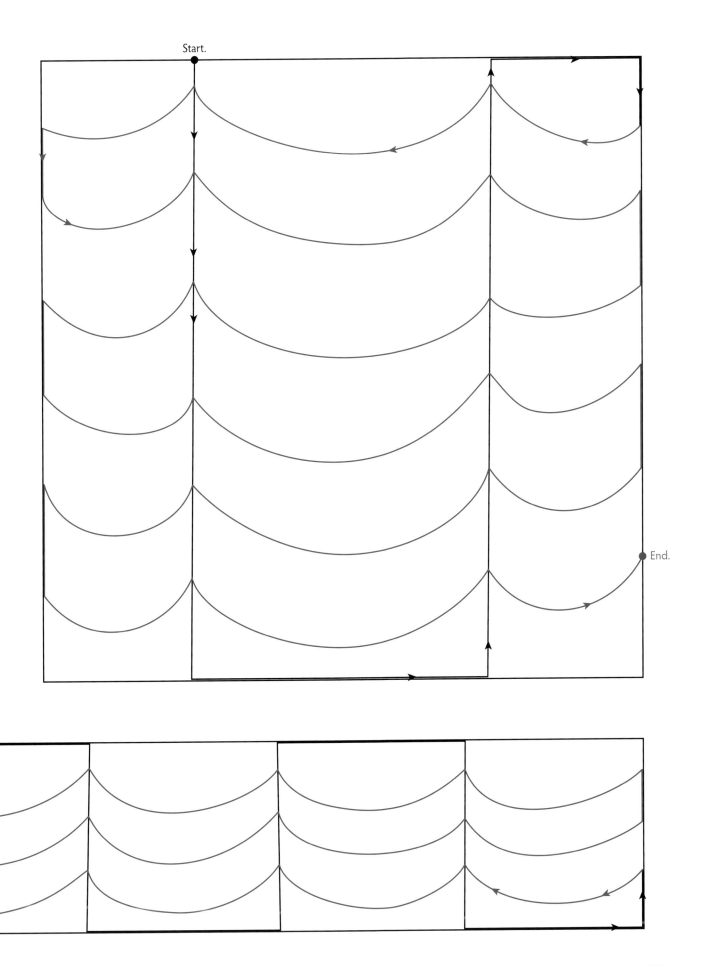

Start.

End.

Hearts on a String

DESIGNED BY DARA TOMASSON

A great design for fairly new quilters, Hearts on a String creates a stitching path to follow. You'll need to be able to stitch hearts in all directions (horizontal, vertical, left, and right), so becoming comfortable with drawing these is very useful. When tracing back along the side of the heart shapes, alternate sides. This will even out the heaviness of the stitching on the trace-back. Play with the heart sizes and line spacing, which will change the look of the design.

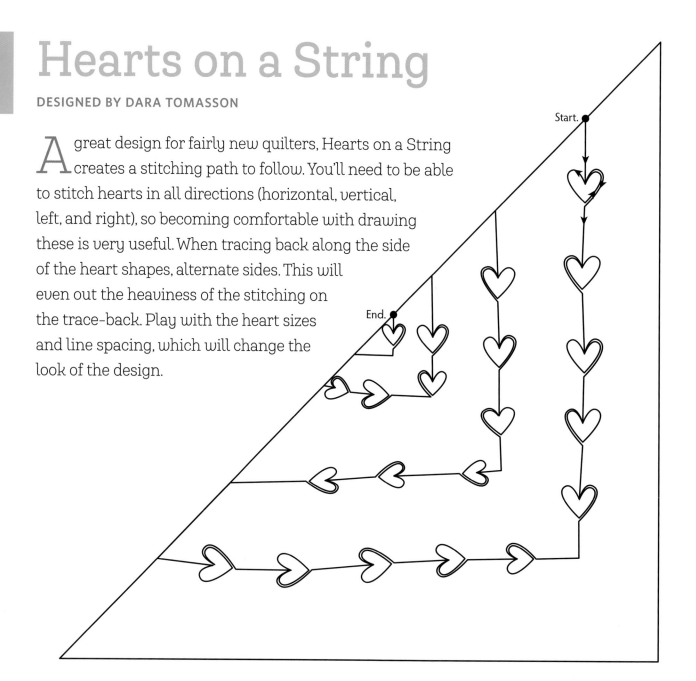

Start.

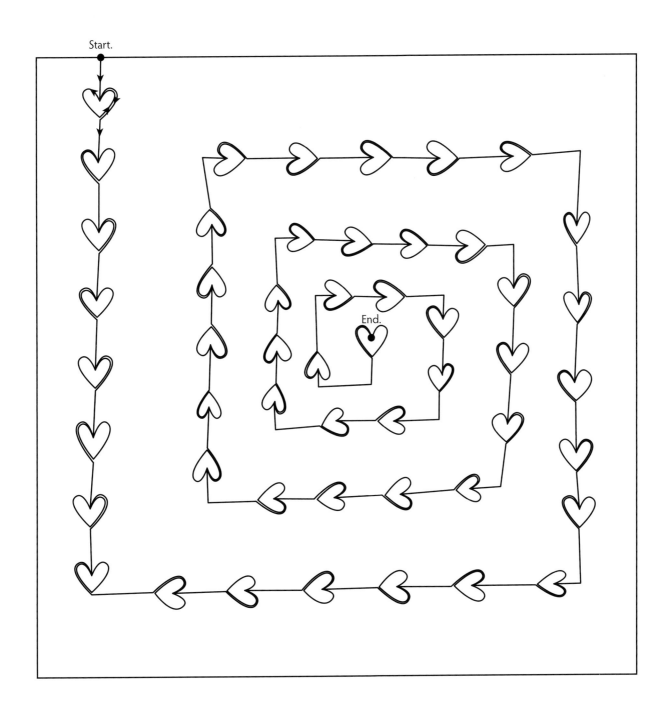

End.

Baby

DESIGNED BY KAREN M. BURNS

Hoping to find a fun and easy way to personalize a baby quilt? Look no further! Experiment by adding additional words and love messages. Cursive writing is easier to quilt than block letters because it has a natural connection between letters, and most people are familiar with the cadence of writing in cursive. Change the words, and you can personalize any quilt—graduation, wedding, birthday, and more!

Start.

Start.

Start.

baby

love

baby name here

End.

ame love

End.

Blooming Cherry

DESIGNED BY LORI KENNEDY

Stitch carefully to keep the Blooming Cherry shapes as symmetrical as possible. For the square block, start by stitching a small circle in the center, and then add leaves on the diagonal lines of the block with the cherries on the horizontal and vertical lines. Keep the border motif symmetrical by adding evenly spaced tick marks where each cherry stem begins. While Blooming Cherry has a modern flair, it looks great on traditional quilts and baby quilts too!

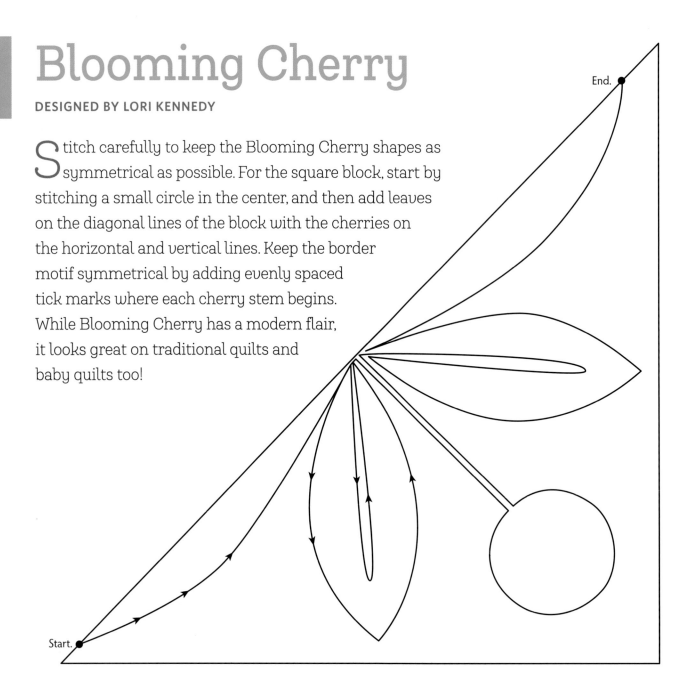

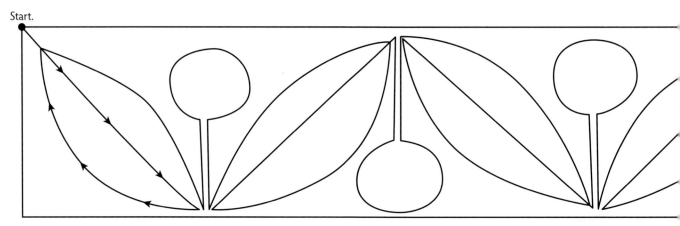

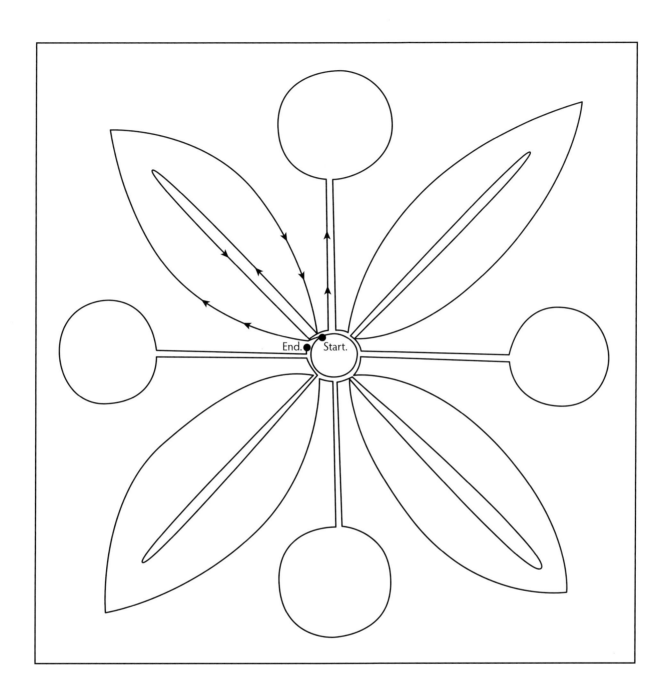

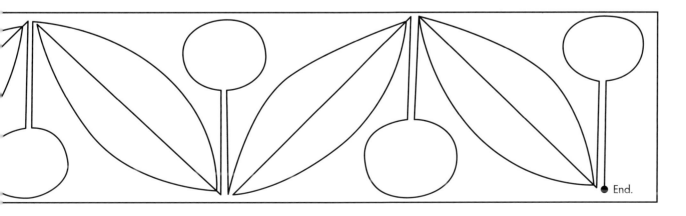

Holiday Lights

DESIGNED BY KARRLYN MARCHUK

Light up a holiday quilt with this simple design that combines ribbons, swirls, and rounded triangles that form the bulbs. Start with a few swirls that connect to the ribbons, then continue into a rounded triangle to create the bulb. Have fun with this design, and make the bulbs as big or small as you like!

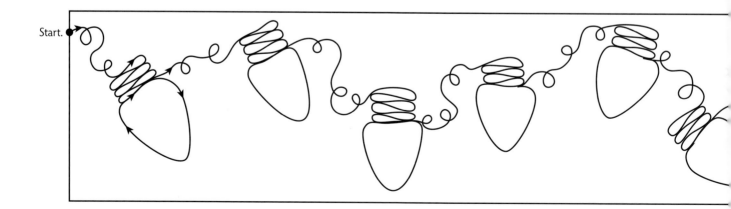

Start.

End.

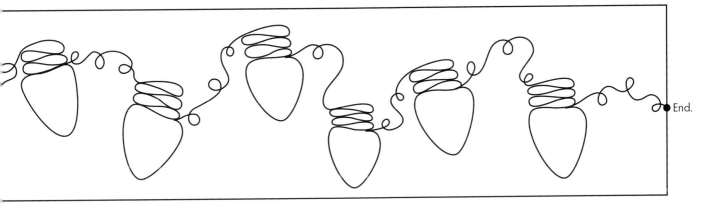

End.

Wild West

DESIGNED BY MELISSA CORRY

Wild West is a perfect filler for cowboys and cowgirls alike! Anyone can stitch Wild West because it incorporates basic loops with the five-pointed stars that we learned to doodle as children. Simply start with some loops and then when you get to a nice open spot, stitch a star. The star will start and finish in the same spot so you can continue stitching more loops to meander over to your next desired star placement. Before you know it, you'll have filled your entire quilt with Wild West quilting goodness.

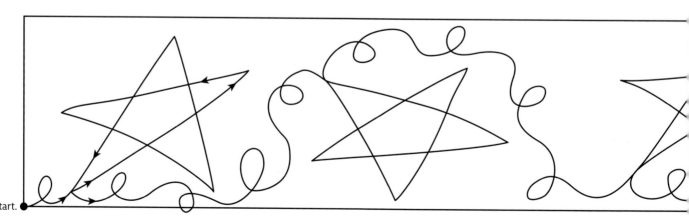

Start.

End.

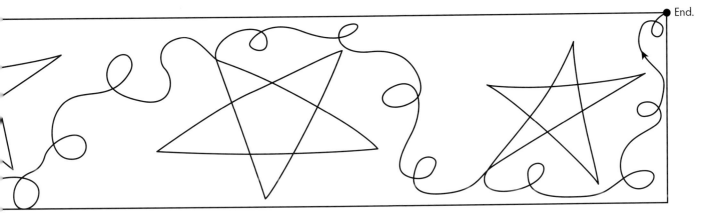

End.

Eagle Feather

DESIGNED BY KRYSTAL JAKELWICZ

Eagle Feather is a beginner-friendly quilting design that stitches quickly and covers a large area. If you need a guide, start by drawing a leaf-shaped outline using an erasable ink pen or chalk. Quilt the feather shaft first—essentially a pointed loop—and then simply follow around the shaft, stitching a leaf shape in a curved, jagged line that peaks at the tip. Make a simple feather, a pair, or a complete border row, curving the feathers in opposite directions.

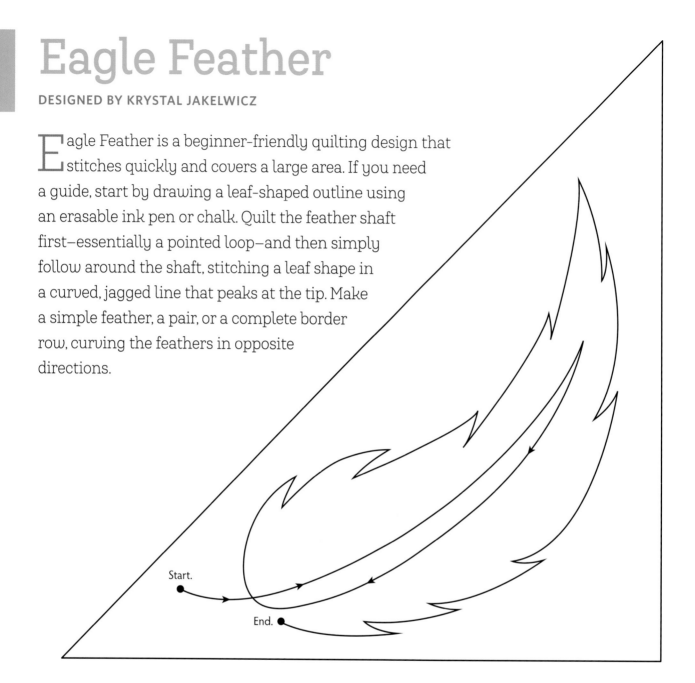

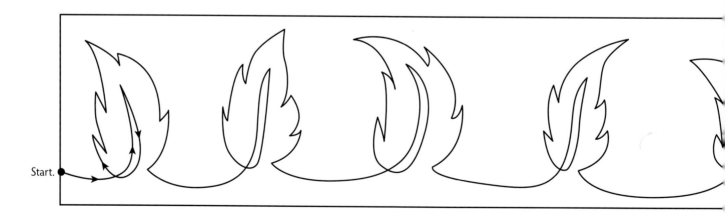

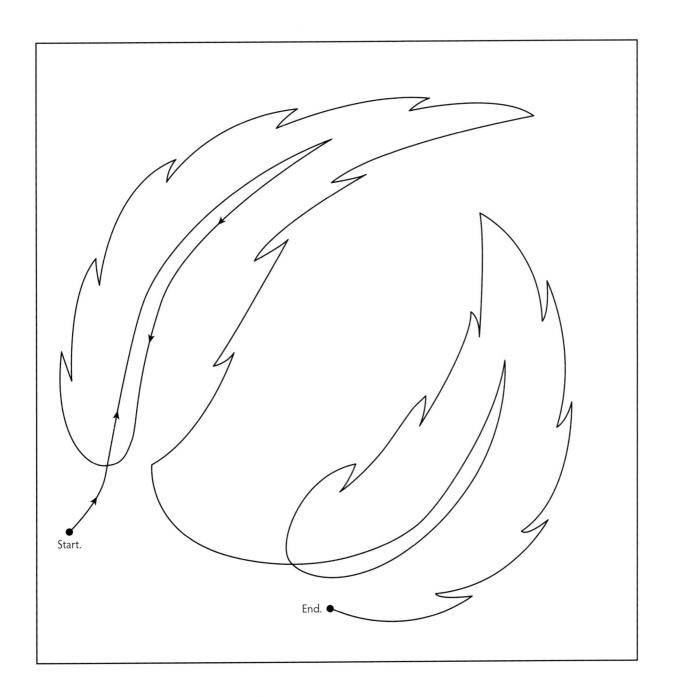

Start.

End.

End.

Peacock Tips

DESIGNED BY DARA TOMASSON

A fairly straightforward design for the free-motion quilter who has experience with swirls, Peacock Tips is simply a swirl with flair! It's ideal for gender-neutral projects. The symmetry of the border offers wonderful texture and design, and using all three versions on a different scale can create interest and variety in a single project.

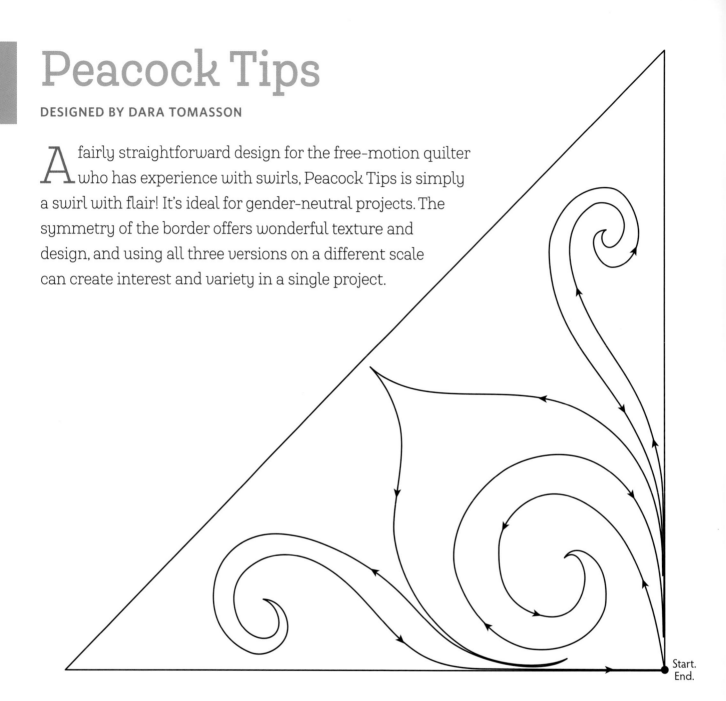

Start.
End.

End.

Start.

Start.

End.

Path to Your Heart

DESIGNED BY CAROLYN MURFITT

A heart lover's dream design, Path to Your Heart cultivates love in every stitch. The sweet, feminine lines beg to be quilted on something perfectly pink. The corner version is particularly appealing in the way the heart motifs appear to grow from bud to blossom along the meandering vine. The lines are easy to follow, the heart shapes don't demand perfection and, with virtually no backtrack stitching, the design offers a clean finish and flow.

Start.
End.

End.

Dog Bones

DESIGNED BY LAURIE GUSTAFSON

Too doggone cute! A loopy line linking various-sized dog bones is just the ticket for finishing Rover's patchwork puppy mat. The lines enter and exit each bone at one end, making it simple to work around one shape and move to the next. And if you're not in the habit of quilting for your furry friend, you just found a reason to start! Of course this design is a perfect way to finish a quilt for any dog-loving humans too!

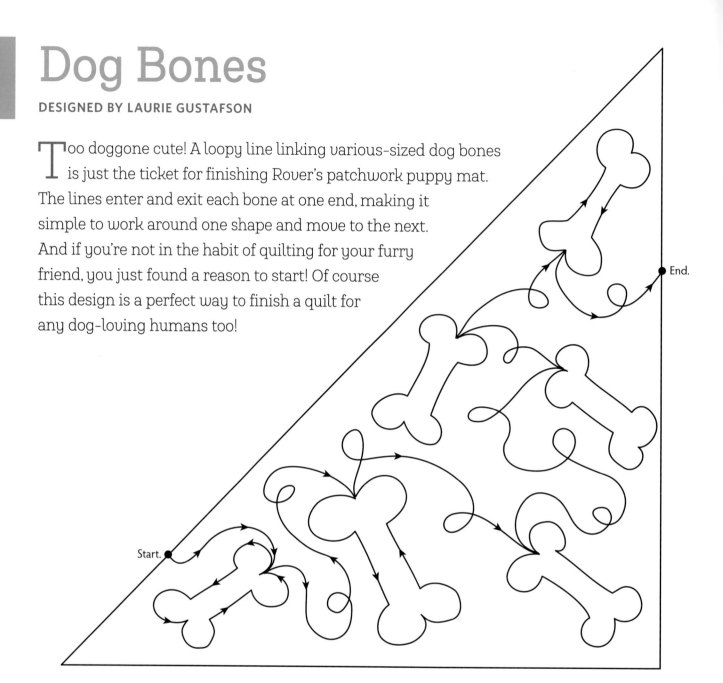

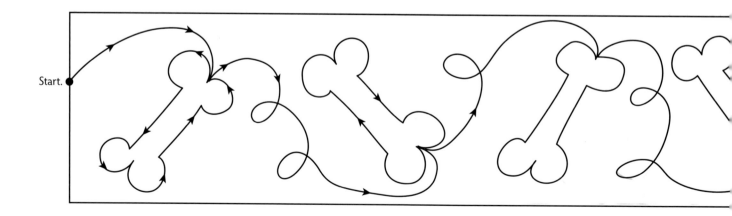

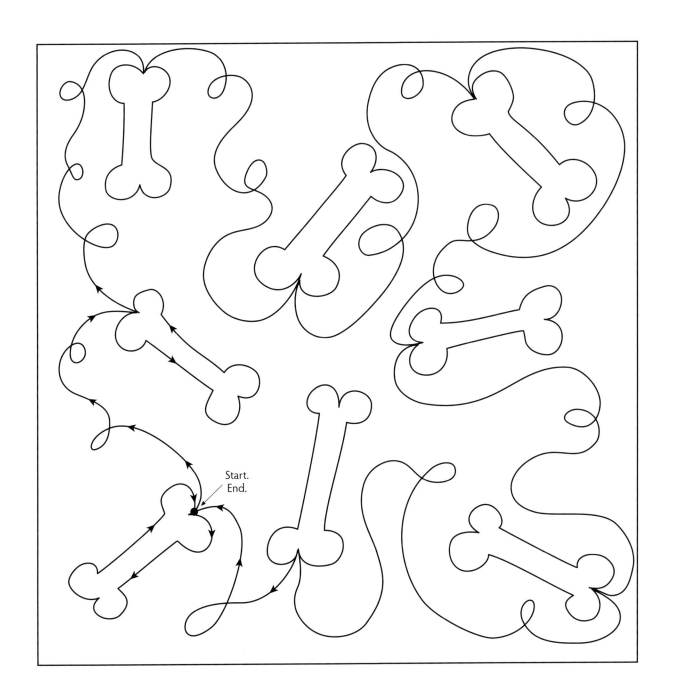

Start.
End.

End.

About the Contributors

Tracey Browning

Constantine Quilts
ConstantineQuilts.com.au

Karen M. Burns

Compulsive Quilting

Melissa Corry

Happy Quilting
HappyQuiltingMelissa.com

Laurie Gustafson

Laurie's Creative Quilting
LauriesCreativeQuilting.com

Maggi Honeyman

Sew Maggi's Quilting
SewMaggisQuilting.com

Krystal Jakelwicz

Let's Quilt Something
LetsQuiltSomething.com

Amelia Johanson

Kelsi Karg

Instagram: @KelsiKarg

Lori Kennedy

TheInboxJaunt.com

Karrlyn Marchuk

Instagram: @karrlynlm

Carolyn Murfitt

FreeBirdQuiltingDesigns.com.au

Vicki Ruebel

Orchid Owl Quilts
OrchidOwlQuilts.com

Rebecca Silbaugh

Ruby Blue Quilts
RubyBlueQuilts.blogspot.com

Dixie Thue

Instagram: @dixiethue

Dara Tomasson

StitchedQuiltingCo.com